MY HEART
BEHIND BARS

LTG Leo Publishing

www.lorribritt.com

ISBN: 978-1-7782517-0-2 (paperback)
ISBN: 978-1-7782517-1-9 (ebook)
ISBN: 978-1-7782517-2-6 (audiobook)

Ordering Information:
Special discounts are available on quantity purchases by corporations, associations, and
others. For details, contact www.lorribritt.com

MY HEART BEHIND BARS

A MOTHER'S JOURNEY OF GRIEF, INCARCERATION, LOVE AND FORGIVENESS

LORRI BRITT

DEDICATION

This book is dedicated to everyone and anyone who has struggled with parenting, growing up, addiction, mental health, grief, feelings of shame or loneliness, or being outcasted. You're not alone—I got you.

CONTENTS

INTRODUCTION

My heart, or pieces of it anyway—my sons—were behind bars. I was unable to see, touch, or talk to them on a regular basis. There were no final goodbyes because they were very much alive, though maybe not well. Their presence was missed daily, and it seemed there was no end to the grief cycle I was in. What I know to be true is that this can happen to anyone. A poor choice and some bad timing, and your heart is behind bars.

It Happens in an Instant

Everything changed that night, when a friend and her son showed up at my door at 2 a.m. explaining that Drake had called her son crying, asking for help. He'd given a street name for them to pick him up, and when they got to the location, the police had apprehended him and he was in the back of the police vehicle. He definitely was not waiting on the street corner as they had expected, and I had no idea what to do next.

Hearts Are Fragile

When my son was arrested, I found most people were unable to wrap their heads around the idea of grief associated with incarceration. They found it difficult to be supportive and often focused more on the crime and the criminal instead of the grief and the griever. It felt like there was more judgment and less compassion. That people were unable to comprehend the pain, the loss, and the heartbreak of things they never experienced or didn't have the capacity to understand. I believe because of this, most people were unable to be supportive or show up in a way I needed. Honestly, most just did not show up at all.

If He Had Died

Had my son died, compassion, empathy, and care would've poured over me; but instead, my grief was dismissed. My heartbreak was just as real as any other loss, yet in society's eyes, it was unacceptable because my son had committed a crime and was in prison.

It's similar to the way society reacts if a drug addict dies of an overdose, expressing thoughts like, "Well, they shouldn't have been doing drugs." When a drunk driver crashes and dies, somehow it is deserved, because they "should've known better."

But the family of that addict or drunk driver is probably heartbroken, and yet they're left to feel alone, in a place where shame is attached to their grief. And because of that, instead of just being able to grieve, they have to defend or deny their own feelings.

And yet no one ought to feel ashamed for loving someone, no matter what that person's choices were...you have every right to cry. You have no need to be embarrassed or ashamed about loving your child, friend, mother, father, or partner— no matter how that grief is viewed by society.

No Compassion, No Grieving

There is much less compassion in the world than I thought— thankfully, I have a friend who understood grief better than I had ever hoped to; she knew that I would not be able to go through the whole process. Not just because of the restrictions placed by the prison walls, but also due to the lack of understand among my social circle and society. She unfortunately had experienced a loss deeper than I can imagine, she understood the process, she knew that closure was a part of it along with support. She knew that I would get stuck in the process.

She was right. I was not able to fully grieve; there was no closure, there was no end to my sense of loss from the time of the arrest to sentencing, to time served, or even in release.

How to Use This Book, or What This Book Is About

I don't want to pull apart the people that didn't show up, wallow in self-pity, or tear down the system (though it has its faults).

This book is to help someone else who may be struggling, lost, and alone in a sea of pain.

To share some very vulnerable times, incredible pain that will, I hope, help someone to understand, so they are able to show up for someone in some capacity even if they don't know what the person is going through.

To let you know that you are not alone, and it's okay to feel sad. It's okay to be angry at everyone and everything for a little bit because the sadness that has consumed your body is so deep that the only way out is anger. Anger is the easier emotion; it enables you to stay standing because it allows you to protect your heart, for if you gave into the sadness you would crumble. Anger is the only emotion you seem to find the ability to understand because anger gives you a false sense of control where the pain from your heartbreak is not fathomable.

It's okay to feel everything you're feeling, even if no one around you understands.

No matter how society perceives your situation or expects you to behave, these emotions are big, and they are real. It is 100 percent okay for you to feel all of your feelings, to be petty, to be angry, to be protective, to be disconnected, to isolate, to salvage what pieces of your heart are still intact, and to do your best to move through the days, because, my friend, this is how we manage when we are trying to survive.

Most of all, it is good to go through the process, to learn to be kind to yourself, leave the self-judgment; there will be enough judgment going on already. And when you move through it, you get to the beautiful place where you have empathy and care even for those that were unable to give it to you.

Always do your best, even on those days when opening your eyes is painful because the thought of what's missing sinks deep within your soul and the extra weight that has sat on your chest makes it harder to breathe, and you haven't even moved yet.

Always show up for yourself, meaning lean into the pain, do

not try to escape it. Learn about yourself and the emotions that are crippling you. Nurture yourself—you are the most important person, even if it doesn't feel like it. You have to dig deep and do the work to take care of you and heal, because if you do not, you are unable to do so for the rest of your family, including your inmate.

One day you're going to open your eyes and you're going to be a better person than you were before this ache took possession of your heart and consumed your body. Because you know that you will always be able to connect with those in grief, even if the situation isn't the same; you know that you can show up for people in a way most cannot, that with your ache you have managed to achieve a kindness, forgiveness, and unconditional care you didn't know existed.

This book is about that loss, that experience, and navigating through the experience of it all to heal deep wounds and find closure, or something similar to it, in order to heal my heart. Because, in the blink of an eye, this can happen to anyone.

I know most people will say, "Well, it won't happen to me, not my kid, not in my life." I totally understand that, and I've heard it from many. And you're right, until it does—the shock that shakes your entire world. I never imagined that I would be writing this book with my children's names as the characters I write about. For a moment when you're reading, imagine your child in place of mine. It's harder when it's your own, it affects you differently. Maybe you will see some similar things, maybe you won't. Maybe you see it in someone else's child, in someone you love and care about. Maybe it helps you to have conversations you didn't think about.

The impact of my sons going to jail affected me as a mom, friend, partner, employee, pretty much every aspect of my life. It shifted my entire world. It was like having a brand-new pair of prescription glasses—how I saw the world prior to my sons going to jail is vastly different than the way I see it now. I pray that you never experience what I went through, that you are always able to view the world in a brighter light, but if you do, I hope that I was able to help by sharing my pain.

ONE

JULY 26

Juuly 26 is an important day for me. My son Drake was born on this day in 1992, and on July 26, 2013, he was arrested. On his 21st birthday, his life changed significantly, and so did mine.

There have been more than a few moments in my life journey with my son where we have encountered some turbulence. Society from a young age had pegged him as difficult, challenging, nonconforming, defiant, a troublemaker, and more. My son has always had a strong will, a determined disposition, and one spitfire spirit. Like every parent, I had a pretty good picture of my child's personality while he was growing up. Like the other parents, I could always see the good in my children—that said, I didn't wear rose-coloured glasses all day, every day. I can call a spade a spade, even with my own children.

I knew early on in our journey of parent and child that we were going to have some lessons and power struggles, and I had some choices to make on parenting.

Those choices start when your child is young. Some are simple, and the goal is to tackle these things early on, so that as our children grow, they are able to make better choices. To make these decision or choices without your assistance or reassurance. You want your child to learn from natural consequences, preferably those not as traumatic as the result of what happened in my son's life on July 26, 2013.

In any case, I believed firmly that my children should be encouraged to formulate and make their own decisions. I tried to let them make the right choices by giving them options or a way out of poor decisions.

Let's say it's winter, and my son was determined to wear shorts to school. So, I could sit and argue with him, or I could encourage him to pack a pair of sweatpants in his backpack.

Sure, the other parents might stare at you and talk about you being a shitty mom because your kid is wearing shorts in the middle of winter and there is snow on the ground. But really, who cares? Let them form their opinion. My son will get cold, realize his poor choice of shorts, and he will have a pair of pants to put on when he's ready.

He learns the lesson on his own, and you move forward. This empowers him, and there's less stress for you as you move along through life. I had a lot of those times with my son. Some were as easy as that, and some not so much.

School was just the beginning for us. There were times when he was very little and I had to drop him off for school, they would have to pull him off me.

He did not want to be there, and he did not want me to leave. It was heartbreaking. I had to go, I had to work, and it sucked. I would leave crying myself, although not in front of him—

I'd be strong and explain he had to go to school.

Yet despite how distraught we both were, I am sure the only message he got was, "I am abandoning you because I have more important things to do." So not the case, though at five or six years old, I am sure those thoughts went through his mind.

It was in these early years that teachers would talk to me about his behaviour. Some conversations I would value as truth, and some I disregarded. To me, it was then that his spirit really started to shine. I would get talks about how he was too outspoken, he wouldn't listen, he was disruptive in class.

They tested him because they thought there must be something wrong with him because he was acting up. I didn't see it that way. It was his personality they objected to. If you talked to him in a manner he didn't like, he would call you on it—meaning he would talk back and would be direct about how you spoke to him. If he felt like you were being mean, he would tell you so; if you made him feel humiliated, he would act out. And if you continually nagged him, he would stop listening. If you couldn't keep his mind engaged and active, he would grow bored and start finding things to amuse himself.

I didn't need a label for him, although most of society did. I heard things like he was on the autism spectrum, he had ADHD, ADD, or something that could label his behaviour or could be corrected, and if not, at least justified. This was how they explained him to me. I may have taken more value in the things that they were saying if someone had given us some direction, action plan, or tools. If they had done more than put a label on a behaviour that they found difficult to deal with. If they would have suggestions on where to go, help to seek, things to do, things to read, places to get guidance, anything that would help me to help him, I may have put more into what they were saying. However, labels are all they had attached to him to justify why it was so difficult for them. A label didn't solve anything; it was simply put on to justify others' behaviours and actions toward the individual.

I am not saying that those things are not true, he may have one of those conditions; it was who he was, label or not. I am not going to deny my son did walk to the beat of his own drum, and still does to this day.

I really started to devalue what they were conditioning him with when he was left behind, forgotten at the school, when his class left on a field trip. He was six years old when he walked out of the washroom to join his class only to realize they had left. His reaction was to walk home rather than go to the principal or someone else at school. His feelings were hurt and he didn't trust any of them, so he returned to the person he did trust: me.

I saw him out of the corner of my eye while I was driving down the road. He was on a back street, so I picked him up, asked what he was doing and why he wasn't off skating with his class. I am a very protective mama bear, and I was not very happy when he said he was left behind.

The anger I had toward the teacher for her irresponsibility of leaving him behind was instant. For him to have little to no faith or trust in the adults at the school where he was left in a situation, he could walk off like that. So many things could have happened to him. He could have been hit by a car, taken by somebody, gotten lost in woods, not made it home, or made it home when I wasn't there.

I don't know how long he had been walking, but when I

picked him up, it was getting close to the end of the school day. I thought how strange it was that no one who went on that field trip called the school to look for him or that the school hadn't notified me that he was unaccounted for.

At any rate, we went to my workplace together. I called my babysitter to come get him from my work since he wouldn't be at the school for her to pick up. It was only after I had Drake calm and taken care of that I called the school to find out what had happened.

His teacher and any other school officials didn't have any idea Drake was missing until then. This was the same teacher who told me how difficult my child was, how hard he was to manage, and how disruptive he was. She noticed those things, but she didn't even notice that he wasn't in class. She had taken her whole class skating, and not once in the course of the day had she noticed that her most challenging student wasn't there.

If a child is supposedly so difficult, and that child is the one that you complain about the most, it strains my belief that you don't even notice if that child is gone. I would certainly know if someone who got under my skin, on my last nerve, was not present.

It made me wonder if she did know he was gone but didn't care enough to find out where he was, because that six-year-old child was so annoying to her. After listening to her complain for months about how many problems he caused for her, I found it disrespectful, ignorant, and shocking that she did not accept any blame for leaving my son behind. In fact, she was angry at me because I filed a complaint about her actions that day, which caused disciplinary action that included some suspension.

That was not the first nor the last time someone had complaints about my son, nor would it be for me showing up to love and support one of my children. The next year, Drake went through a phase where I couldn't get him to wear clothes. Everything bugged his skin, he said. The inside of the socks bothered his toes, his shirts were too rough, his pants were too tight, so he didn't wear any. This lasted for three months. I was told by his pediatrician that he possibly had Asperger's, then possibly lupus. No one knew for sure.

I home-schooled him in that time frame. It was challenging for me, because I was a shift worker at BC Ferries, working as a catering and first aid attendant. But it was what it was, and I did what we had to do to move through this phase. And as I felt that it would, this passed, and I figured that I just had a child who felt like he didn't fit in and was very sensitive.

Because of that, he found a way to stay home, to make himself feel more comfortable. He found a way to stay where he felt safe. To this day, he wears non-stitch socks, loose fitting clothes, soft fabrics. I'm sure there is some label for this, though I cannot tell you what it is called, and I would ask, what does it matter? It is who he is.

Where I am going with all of this is that from the time he was quite young until the July night my friend came to my door, I knew he was going to have some challenges.

He showed me that there are things that he is uncomfortable with in the world and that the world was uncomfortable with parts of him. Neither would conform to the other's expectations; the world is not ready to adapt, and he was unable to.

All of this led to many challenges in school with the old teaching module, where they had one set curriculum that didn't work for the mass majority of students—it was only successful for approximately 20 percent, my son not being one of that percentage. For Drake, by fifth grade, he was pretty much done with the system. He had never felt comfortable going to school, he was struggling with his learning, he was bored, and with that he became more disruptive in classes. But fortunately, Drake was a solid friend, and his support for one particular friend kept him in school.

His friend Joe ended up in a wheelchair after an unknown virus caused him to lose the ability to use his legs from the hips down.

When Drake found out, he asked if the bottles he had been

collecting to pay for a BMX race with his sister could be do-
nated to Joe as his contribution to a fundraiser for a wheelchair. I dropped off three truckloads of bottles to that drive.

Drake, true to his heart, took it upon himself to make sure
Joe was cared for and included. He pushed Joe's wheelchair
around on school outings, looked out for him while on field
trips, mastered video games together, and joined wheelchair
basketball so that he could play with Joe. He was my son's
best friend, and Joe being in a wheelchair wasn't going to
change that.

Because Drake was always with Joe, the teacher's aide as-
signed to Joe would also help Drake. I really believe that's
one of the only reasons Drake made it to high school. The
aide helped Drake by recognizing what he needed assistance with. She was very kind to Drake, and she helped both
boys with every subject, which also helped Drake stay more
grounded. With just the two of them to focus on, he got the
attention he needed to learn.

Yet there were still plenty of bumps along the way, inside and
outside of school. In eighth grade, he was caught shoplifting, as many eighth-grade students do. I share this with you
as a parent to parent. Because if it's your first time around,
you feel embarrassed and ashamed then realize that it is a
pretty common behaviour around this age. I am unsure if
it's because it is the first year of high school, they are a small

fish in a big pond again, or if they are trying to impress and fit in with others. It's been my experience that many eighth graders will steal some small items—girls seem to gravitate toward makeup and boys to junk food.

Many kids show remorse if they are caught, promise never to do it again, that sort of thing. But when Drake was caught shoplifting some junk food from the grocery store and the police were called, there was no crying, there was no drama or theatricals (unlike when his sister was caught)—he stayed tight-lipped and acted like he didn't care.

He seemed like he was trying to keep his emotions restricted and closed. His behaviour was so much different than his sister's, despite the fact that they had the same upbringing. He distrusted the very idea of revealing any vulnerability. So when the store manager brought in the police, he wouldn't give the police the satisfaction of showing he was afraid of being arrested. He already had a distrust for authority and there was no way he was going to let them see he was upset.

It was at the age of 15 to 16 that his group of friends changed, and things escalated. He was spending less time with Joe and more time with dope smokers and partiers.

One time, I got a call to pick him up from a party, and when I arrived, I was directed out to a ditch where I found him incoherent. He obviously couldn't tell me what he'd taken to end up in this shape. Thankfully, the young, concerned girl that called for me to come pick him up said she believed he drank a 26-ounce Captain Morgan's rum and smoked some dope.

On the way home, he kept rubbing his tummy and moaning, still unable to speak clearly. I kept talking to him to see if he would respond, and as I am pulling up the driveway, I am thinking something isn't right, this feels off. As my thoughts go through my mind, he vomits all over the car. I immediately put the car in reverse and head to the hospital.

Initially I could carry him out of the car by scooping him out of the seat, except he had to get sick, so I had to stand him up. After that, I had to literally half carry him, half drag him standing straight up against me from the hospital parking lot toward the hospital admittance area, which wasn't easy. In spite of how hard it was, I was sure we could make it across the endless lot, but sadly we did not. He had to get sick again and then lay down on the ground. There was no way I was able to pick him back up.

At that point, he was directly behind a car, so I couldn't leave him there while I went into the hospital for help or to get a wheelchair, and I couldn't lift him. He was not moaning anymore or moving, it was hard to see if he was breathing. Being a former first aid attendant, I checked his pulse. Nothing, so I checked his other arm, nothing.

Already fighting my rising panic, I checked his carotid, and thank God, it was there. I was grateful; however, it did not ease the urgency and panic of needing to get him inside the hospital and the challenge of my current situation.

I still didn't know how to get him inside the hospital. There was no one around, no one to call to, no one to ask for help. A car passed me as I was checking Drake's vitals, then it passed me again as I was trying to lift him. I was a bit worried when it was coming for the third time, but the driver stopped and asked if I needed assistance. I quickly said that I did—I have never been so relieved.

There were three U.S. Navy servicemen in the car. One was ordered to go get a wheelchair, one stood ground, while the one in charge talked to me about what was going on. I explained that I thought my son had alcohol poisoning, that I thought he was in danger. I am sure he thought I might be an overreacting mom as he checked for a pulse the same way I had, and he, too, was relieved to find the carotid.

Like myself, he realized Drake was in a bad way and told me to go inside and tell the hospital we are coming. He didn't bother to wait for that wheelchair—instead he picked Drake up and carried him while I ran ahead.

The triage nurse wasn't all that responsive once she found out that drugs and alcohol were involved with the patient that was going to be coming in. The urgency of it all dissipated. At least until the Naval officer walked in carrying my son and told her that Drake needed immediate assistance. She, like the officer and I, did vital checks and admitted him immediately. You will encounter this a fair amount when you are dealing with someone who is struggling with drugs and alcohol—the symptoms they have get overlooked or passed off as a product of the drug or alcohol use. One time, it took three different doctors until one was able to look past my son's addictions to give him a diagnosis of shingles. I don't believe it is because they don't care, I believe it is because they see it so often—the ones looking for a fix, issues to get medication to get them high—and eventually they all get painted with the same brush. The doctors and nurses that are continually exposed to the exploit of the addict doing what they can to get something to make them feel better or numb what they are feeling. Much like the addict, the medical care folks become numb to it—they see the same thing over and over, that they get clouded by the fact the person is an addict and at times are unable to see past that. Just like an overweight person who comes in with complaints about lack of breath and low energy, the issues are placed on their weight. Lose weight, issue solved. That's the solution until they're rushed into emergency because they are bleeding internally from cancer with a blood count so low they can go into cardiac arrest, and the next thing you know they are having life-saving surgery that has nothing to do with being overweight. Much like the addict where all problems are placed on the addiction, the extra weight is the focus for someone with extra pounds on them. Everyone judges a book by its cover, but reading the book's pages allows you to learn. Meaning our perception of a situation can cloud the real issue.

Ultimately, Drake was all right, though it was a very long night for me, and unfortunately it was the first of many. We spent all night in emergency; you're grateful that your child is okay, but it doesn't make the circumstances any less upsetting.

Your first thoughts are not that your child has a problem; there is no expectation that you will be dealing with this situation or something similar again. He made no promises to stop behaving this way, and I didn't ask because in my mind we wouldn't be encountering this situation again. I asked him why he was drinking and why drink so much? He said he had not intended to; he was a bit uncomfortable and he thought maybe he drank too fast and it hit him all at once. With the natural consequences to his overindulging—trying to function the next day feeling so very unwell, the shame of having to face the people from the party, and losing 250 dollars to pay to clean the vomit out of my car—I figured the lesson was learned.

Did I expect him to do it again? Absolutely not. A onetime deal is what I thought! Did I have some blinders on, though? Probably. He was remorseful as well as embarrassed that he drank so much that he was out of control and blacked out.

Yet there were at least three other times that I had to go to emergency with Drake due to drugs or alcohol, and I know a couple of other times he had to go with friends. Once he did mushrooms, passed out, and went into convulsions. He lost control of bodily functions. The doctor told him that his brain couldn't handle the hallucinogenic drug. For whatever reason, that rang true for my son and he stayed away from hallucinogenic drugs, for the most part at least.

Around this point in time, one has to really look at the situation for what it truly is. As a parent, you have to take off your rose-coloured glasses and look at the behaviours and actions of your child as well as some of your own. To make a poor choice once or twice is pretty standard in teenage/young adult life, but the number of times that I ended up in emergency or picking Drake up, I had to accept that he had a problem. For myself, I also had to look at how I was justifying his behaviour and actions. Did I have shame attached to it? Was I in denial? Was I making excuses for him because he came from a broken home? Because I worked shift work? Did I enable his behaviour because I knew he had learning disabilities and struggled with things? Did I allow it to be more accepting because I knew that it could be a family issue? This is probably one of the hardest places to be as a parent/partner because you love these individuals so much that you tend to want to help them, take care of them, and lots of times we have our own emotional wounds attached to it all. You tend to not want to see it all clearly because you end up having to make hard decisions, and with all the mess that is already happening, it can feel very daunting and too much work—another thing for you to have to do in an already overwhelming, emotional situation.

I absolutely would've loved to get him help, set him up in a program for mental health and addiction. Unfortunately, there was no real help available for teenagers or young adults. You can't make your child go for treatment; with Canada's health laws, we are unable to enforce involuntary treatment for a minor. Even if I could have forced my son into a treatment facility or program, there is nothing specifically for boys or men in terms of that kind of support group anyway.

My kids have always been my driving force, and being their only voice at times, I did advocate within my union for teenage treatment as well as support for mental health and addiction for boys and men. Fighting for a "men's only" issue comes with its challenges due to past history; however, seeing how lost my boys were within our society, I had to fight for some place for them, some place better than behind prison walls.

The Women's Rights movement, I feel, has done great things for women: they have safe havens, treatment centres, as well as meetings specific for women only. Women have gained more control and power of choice than they have had, which is beautiful. Unfortunately, there are no haven facilities for boys or men, nowhere for them to go for support or some sense of stability if they happen to be in an abusive situation. They have advanced with having treatment and meetings for men only now; however, there are still no teenage treatment facilities or much in the way of support options for struggling families of teens.

At the time I struggled with my boys, there was little to no help. Families for Addiction Recovery is an outreach charity that was established in 2017. It was established by successful moms struggling with their own children's mental health and addiction issues. They have great support staff and a ton of resources. You can visit their website at http://www.far-canada.org or call them at 1-855-377-6677. They, like myself, understand that your hands are tied. You are unable to force your child into treatment if they are a minor, and as an adult, it has to be their choice. The very lovely thing about these moms is they built something to help other moms/dads/siblings to not feel so crazy and alone. It's very frustrating. Society wants to hold you responsible for your child's actions, but they offer no support to help you help your child.

Some of Drake's issues with drugs and alcohol could be due to genetics; mental health and addiction seems to be a family trait. Not only did his father, Mark, have his own issues with substance abuse, but we also seemed to have a history between both sides of our families. Mental health and addiction seemed to affect the mass majority of us. Mark and

I were divorced, and while Drake didn't see his father's issues daily because he lived with me, a child is exposed no
matter how hard we try to protect them. The effects of substance abuse come through no matter how hard you try to
protect your children from it—missed time, odd behaviour,
ultimately they feel the effects. I was not one to say mean or
cruel things about his dad, I firmly believe the relationship
between them was for them to figure out. My job was to
keep Drake safe and exposure as minimal as possible, not to
cultivate my negative opinions about his dad's behaviour on
to him, which was tough when at 16, he decided that he was
going to go live with his dad.

When Drake decided to make the decision to live with his
father, I was staying in Fort Bragg, California, temporarily for
a month-long course that I needed for business knowledge.
My family wasn't able to come with me, so they had to stay
home. My husband, Jason, drove me to California, which is
how Drake ended up at his dad's. With Mark being clean
and sober for the last seven years, it was a great opportunity
for them to spend time together. When Jason came home,
they decided that staying with Mark was a better choice for
both Drake and Jason. While time passed when I was at the
course, Drake decided living with his dad was what he wanted for him and Chris to do permanently.

I was angry at them all for making a major life decision without me. My feelings were hurt and, to be honest, I felt like

I had no control over my family life. I knew that Mark and Drake needed to have time to bond and build their relationship. I love my son's dad, and I know he loves our children; however, with the way Drake had been behaving and making poor choices that very much resembled some of Mark's older poor choices, coupled with the sense that Mark's sobriety was coming to an end, I didn't feel that them living together was best. Topped with Christopher in trouble with the law, as I found out, and a warrant for his arrest, I felt like this was a poor decision for all of them.

The time he spent with his father was really the least of my worries and was fairly short lived. Unfortunately, Mark relapsed, Chris with much convincing turned himself into the police for the warrant that was out, and Drake came back home, sort of. At our home, Drake was always out, and I was getting calls at all hours of the night or early mornings, calls from him, calls from others concerned about him, and/or calls from the police who had picked him up. You're probably reading that and thinking, "Wow, police are nice in Canada to call you." The reality is that I was able to go get him from the police station because he was a minor, but once someone is an adult, you're no longer allowed that privilege.

The lack of sleep that I had over those years were completely exhausting: the continual phone calls to pick Drake up, not sleeping because your nights are filled with worry and concern, or dealing with shitty behaviour was very trying and definitely taking their toll, not only on myself; it was putting a strain on my marriage to Jason. Jason would ask me to turn the ringer off on the phone at night, to not go and get him if he called, and to let Drake deal with the consequences of his poor choices on his own. I wasn't able to accommodate my husband's request. I was not at that stage of turning my phone off and letting the chips fall where they may. I had a couple of situations where if I had not got my son, he may not be with us today. You and you alone will decide when enough is enough.

You have to be okay with the decision you are making. If I choose to not go and get my son or ignore his phone call and something happens to him, I have to be the one to be okay with my choice. If I ignored my son's call because my husband would be upset or angry if I did, or I did it to please my husband and something happened to my son, well your marriage is over anyway, at least mine would be. I would undoubtedly blame my husband and therefore is the reason I only turned off the ringer when I was ready. You need to have respect, communication, and hopefully come to some understanding in your marriage.

It is not an easy journey; I now know why so many marriages fall apart during situations like this. Not only do you need compassion, care, and understanding in your marriage, you need it for yourself. You need to find compassion for the crazy you feel, the judgment and misunderstanding that comes with trying to keep yourself afloat while pulling up the concrete block (your addict) so you both don't drown, or getting to a place of letting it go so you don't drown. They have groups you can attend. Al-Anon is a good one; it's for a person needing support to help you with the frustration and loneliness of dealing with someone in addiction. It might help you set some boundaries; your addict can and will cross the line every time, so honestly, the boundary setting is for you. They have lots of groups out there for codependency, alcoholics, drug addicts, and those that live with them. I would recommend counselling for yourself; it's one of the most important things you can do. You may want to do a bit of marriage counselling if you can't get on the same page. That was my life for a few years. Late nights, early mornings, little sleep to no sleep. Drinking and trouble, court appearances. It seemed like Drake had issues with everyone: family, friends, and the police.

He even managed to get a hit put on him. He'd had a fight with the grandson of a woman who had dealt with enough in her lifetime to break most of our hearts. She had lost a daughter and so much more, she had no tolerance for someone hurting her family. Strange behaviour that one who won't tolerate abuse yet implements it onto another with some sort of justification that it is okay. Thankfully, that was resolvable. Drake's dad talked to her, and they sorted it out with the family. It was like my life had become very surreal; I was in it yet separated like it wasn't really mine. Like I was watching some heart-wrenching demise of a woman that looked a lot like me but how the hell did it get here, a hit on my son! Seriously how was it so out of control and so far from my reality and yet here it was, my life.

I don't know 100 percent what starts the drug or alcohol use (any addiction for that matter). While talking with my ex-husband Mark, we talked about self-esteem, self-worth, and the issues we have within our own minds. How hanging out with the rougher more party crowd allowed one to not feel as bad about themselves. Doing drugs and alcohol allowed him to numb unwelcoming emotions and escape the imprisonment of his own thoughts. I am not sure if that resonates with all, however, it seems to with the people I know, including my boys.

People wonder why you do not give up. I had many people tell me that I had to let them hit rock bottom. I always found that an interesting and yet very annoying statement. I mean really let them get so far down and watch, don't do anything, just let them spiral. To me its like handing over the keys to someone who has never drove before and saying drive, when you hit the wall that is when you know to stop, you might be dead but hey you stopped. You don't just throw out a lifeline when someone hits bottom. You throw out a lifeline at all opportune moments, whenever you can, however often you can because everyone's bottom is different and for many it's death. You can't help them once they are dead. For myself, I have always thought it unnecessary to wait for someone to reach rock bottom. Rock bottom could be a first-time use. For some reason your child/friend/loved one decides they are going to try a drug, maybe smoke a joint, innocent enough; however, it's laced with something stronger than their body can handle and that is it…gone forever. Are people going to be okay with that? Satisfied with rock bottom? No, people say it and it's the ones that are not living it. You cannot rescue them; that I know! That is the point they are trying to make with the rock bottom statement; however, it doesn't adequately state its purpose. I was not one to idly stand by and wait for death to claim them and I found it beyond irritating when someone suggested I ought to.

What is a lifeline, you wonder. It all starts with uncomfortable, yet necessary conversations. Talks about addiction, family behaviours and traits that get passed down from generation to generation. Things that become acceptable within a home and classified as normal but really play a negative outcome on your standard of living. Talks about the use of drugs and alcohol and the negative impact it can have with using them. Talks about escaping reality by using drugs and alcohol. Seeing behavioural changes and inquiring about them. Talking about the challenges they may be having in life. Dealing with mood swings and finding ways to learn coping skills. Lifelines are not you running out to rescue the addict, they are boundaries and stability. Standing beside them when they are most vulnerable without shame. A lifeline can be as simple as saying I love you at a time when they feel the most unlovable. A lifeline is something they can grasp onto to help themselves up, something solid and grounded, and for the most part that was me.

The climb up from a short distance down is a lot easier than from the bottom. The moments you can reach out is usually when a situation has just happened, and the person feels vulnerable or remorseful—the remorse lifeline, I like to call it. Sometimes they grasp it, they climb and hopefully they make it to the top; however, if they slip again, hopefully it isn't too far down. This can become a very unhealthy spot for you at times. Are you doing too much? Are you doing all the work? Is it helping? Am I enabling, encouraging poor behaviour? Am I making it worse or better? When is enough, enough? As I stated before, you and you alone will know. My way of understanding it was like this: You can lead a horse to water, you can not force them to drink. If you are unable to walk and you're trying to drag yourself to get the horse to water, you are doing too much. I know many people say it is when your life becomes unmanageable. I laugh a little; with an addict in your life…it is always unmanageable.

We have had a few of these in our time, Drake and I; some of them felt more successful than others. Some, I think he had learned and grew from and in all honestly, I grew from all of them. At other times, it seemed like we ended up in the same place we had before, more knowledge and understanding yet right at a place that seemed remarkably familiar.

But the point of all these stories is this: Drake had troubles before, he was doing some of the same, living with me yet not really being present in the house, not working because socializing and partying had taken priority to any other process of day-to-day standards of life, he had given up everything for one thing—addiction. But the night of his 21st birthday, when my friend and her son showed up at my door, that was different, even if I didn't realize it.

There was no sleep after they arrived at my door at 2 a.m., or the rest of the weekend for that matter. The weird thing was I wasn't overly shocked when my friend knocked on my door; I already knew something wasn't right. I had been tossing and turning and already awake when they arrived.

So, I stayed up pacing and waiting until I could phone the police station to find out what had happened. Not that it was much help.

At 21, he was an adult, and due to privacy laws, as well as an ongoing investigation, they could tell me nothing. They couldn't even tell me that they had him, even though I knew they did.

As parents, it would seem to me that no matter what age our

children get, we somewhat feel the need to be involved, that we are important and a main character in their lives; however, one of the biggest lessons I learned through this experience with my boys is that as important as we may feel, we are in their life, we are no longer a main character in the movie role of our child's life.

It is difficult to let go of the spotlight when you don't realize that you're even trying to stay in it. It progresses so slowly over time, the shift, the change that you're unaware it's happening until it happens. In the beginning of their lives we are it, the main character, centre stage, all the lights on us, all of the lines ours. Then we become the secondary act, the sidekick, if we are lucky. And before we know it, we are no longer a main stage character at all. Instead, we become a walk-on in the background of the movie. Next thing you know, you're sitting in the front row of the theatre, not even *in* the movie anymore. You graduate to the middle row seats and eventually you are at the back of the theatre, yelling at the main character on screen—who, though he is your child, can't hear you as you scream at him not to turn around, or to look, or stop, or go, or run.

You can see what's coming, you know what's going to happen, and yet you can do nothing about it except watch and be there for when they need you. But at that moment, when I waited to see why the police were holding Drake, I still believed I was a main character, I was his MOM and after all didn't that give me some clout? Apparently not, and doesn't that get your knickers in a knot.

When I felt it was a reasonable time to finally be able to phone the Royal Canadian Mounted Police (RCMP), they wouldn't even tell me they had him. There is a part of you that is instantly enraged because you are well aware they have him, and then there is a part of you that hopes against hope that maybe he was let go, it was all some kind of a misunderstanding.

I held on to that hope as slight as it might be and proceeded to call the RCMP for a second time. I told them that I wanted to report a missing person. I told them I hadn't been able to contact my son in over 24 hours, that it wasn't his normal behaviour, that it was extremely odd for him not to show for his birthday, and that I was worried something had happened to him. All very true information, and with that I would be able to find out for sure if they still had him in custody.

It sounds like a mixed-up way to get the information that you already know; however, it is the way the system is set up. An associate of mine told me that she thought I was playing the system, and that I was lying to get information that I wasn't entitled to. Wrap your head around that for a moment: my son is arrested, I am not entitled to know until they charge him with something, and even then because he is an adult they do not have to notify you as the parent. I am frantic with worry and apparently I am in the wrong for getting information she feels I'm not entitled to, wondering if she would feel the same if it was her son. I don't feel the same way; I say I was smart enough to figure out a way to get the information that I needed to release the breath I had been holding and take in some new air. In that moment, I realize breathing is a lot harder when the wind is knocked out of you, not physically but with the simplicity of words, "I'm sorry, Mrs. Britt, you cannot file that missing person's, because we have your son in custody." And so you breathe again, and along with your second breath of released air so goes your slight bit of hope.

The police have no problem phoning family members to try to get information from you about the person they have or are looking for; example being, they called me to ask if I knew where Christopher was yet wouldn't tell me why they had Drake in custody. They did tell me that Christopher was the co-accused, yet we have no idea what they are being accused of, no idea what charges are being laid. So not knowing the severity of what they are being accused of makes one reluctant to communicate. Why am I supposed to trust the police officer on the phone? Why would I trust him when they don't trust me? They have already painted me with a brush of what kind of person I am because they have my son in custody, much like most of society they have already formed a belief. I understand that they are doing their job, and a difficult one at that; however, some compassion for the non-accused could be taken into consideration. I don't know the stats on how often people lie to the police or hide the criminal; I would like to believe that most people do the right thing; however, I can tell you, with the harsh tone and unrealistic expectations they placed on me. It did nothing to help them get any information from me, even though I had nothing to share. I became as tight-lipped as they were. I think it is important to know here that you are angry, bitter, and all around pissed off. This is day one of finding out my son has been arrested and that they are looking for Christopher, that's it. Talk about out of control. It is like a mass wrecking ball has just smashed through your home and the insurance company has told you to hang tight they will be with you in a day or two. SURE, NO PROBLEM…it's only a massive storm as the water and debris invade my home and create more destruction, with no protection I will sit in my destroyed home and wait. That's what its like waiting to find out why they have your children or are looking for your children to place into custody.

I had no problem using the system that they set in place for me to figure out where my son was to find some sort of peace. From there on you have to do your own investigating until the police tell you what they are willing to tell you. I had to phone people, asking what they had heard, asking if they knew what was happening, reaching out to everyone and anyone that might have some idea.

This is one of the difficult parts of an experience like this, the not knowing—you're like a frickin' mushroom sitting in the dark, feeding on shit. The police will not give you anything until they want to do so; you can't speak to your child, you can't get information to anyone or from anyone, you can't get anyone to see your child. Your child is now an adult, and as much as you may think you know what your child wants or what your child needs, you no longer are able to make those decisions.

You can't even send in a lawyer, because your child may have already been appointed one. So instead, you're powerless, and you find yourself angry, frustrated, worried, and then right back to pissed off.

"I am his mom, and you can't tell me why you arrested him? You can't let me talk to him? Well, what do I have to do, wait to read about it in the f***ing paper?" It's a bad sign when you're cursing at the RCMP.

Your own language lets you know that you are angrier than you are allowing yourself to believe you are and at this point you are not even sure who you're angry with or at. Your child? The RCMP? Yourself? Prepare yourself for a whole new kinda crazy.

That day, the RCMP only replied by taking my name and number so that they could get someone to call me. At first, I was relieved. I'd know something soon.

But then I learned more than I bargained for. The serious crime investigator called.

TWO

CHRISTOPHER

When the serious crime investigator called, he wasn't asking me about Drake, or calling to give me any information about our current situation. He was calling because he wanted to know if I knew where Christopher was. Christopher, my 21-year-old, was the second suspect in the criminal investigation that he was working on. The investigation that I still had no details on. He told me they had yet to locate Christopher, but he was very much involved, told me if I should happen to hear from my son to notify him right away. I ought to have known that he was involved; the boys were always together. You could not find one without the other. The only time they spent apart was when Christopher went to federal prison at 18 for assault.

Christopher was like a son to me. While I hadn't given birth to him, he was one of my children, nonetheless. He holds a special place in my life. He'd come into our lives as a very young man. He came from a broken home, his biological dad was in and out of prison, his once somewhat stable mother was now a heroin street person, and his stepdad tried hard; however, he had his own demons to deal with. Chris had been through too much in his young life and came with a heart that ached to be cared for. I remember once sitting at the dining room table while we were talking about life—Christopher, Drake, and I—when, out of the blue Christopher said, "You know how you tell Kaylee and Drake that you love them infinity?"

"Yes," I said.

He replied, "I would like something like that. I don't want it to be that same *love you infinity*, that's for them; I'd like us to have something, though."

It melted my heart. I have always said to him, "I love you much," so, I suggested that be our thing, and from that day forward it was. I would say it on the phone, when he left the house, if I dropped him off, and also when I wrote him letters. It was one of these moments when it hit me that he so desperately wanted and needed love. His upbringing was different from Kaylee and Drake's. They had always had the stability of me—I'm not saying that I am super mom and the most stable human on the planet; however, I wasn't an addict. I was present in their day-to-day life. I had a good government job, kept a roof over their heads and food in their bellies, and for the majority of the time growing up they were happy.

That wasn't the case for Christopher, which is I'm sure why he ended up with us. One of the things that I love about him was that he appreciated my time, valued the fact that I was around. He appreciated and valued all the ways I showed up for him no matter how he was living, where he was living, or how he was doing. To be honest, Chris was usually happy to see me, whether he was doing well, in prison, or on the streets.

When we were building our late teen/young adult relationship, he would tell me lies. I would call him on it. He would carry along with his lie and then later I would get angry because I would find out that he for sure had lied. It could sometimes be the stupidest thing, like not admitting if he had been partying with anyone, including Drake, the night before, or more serious things like using drugs.

For example, I would ask him about his night, if he had done drugs. He would tell me about his night then deny drug use. I would push a little harder, about drug use, and he would deny, deny, deny. The truth would come out, and usually that meant I was not a happy lady once it was proven he had lied to me. Not that I would be happy about the drug use; however, it would open us up for some honest conversation.

Drake used to always say to him, "I don't know how she knows or how she finds out, but dude, you have to stop lying to her because she is always going to find out. You might as well just tell her the truth right from the start. She's more inclined to help you if you tell her the truth."

It took Chris awhile because it wasn't what he was used to; however, it did get to the point where he would just be honest about what was happening.

My relationship with Christopher was motherly right from the start. He reminded me of Drake; they were two peas in a pod, with Chris being a bit more standoffish and reserved. I had many a people ask me if I thought Chris was a bad influence on Drake, or vice versa. I will share my belief with you—I am not saying it is your truth, the truth, or anything other than it is my truth; take from it what you will and discard if not needed—I do not believe that either were a bad influence on each other, I believe that people have matching pictures, vibes, energy, whatever you want to call it. Like socializes with like, you know the old saying birds of feather flock together. They could have not hung out, yet they would have found someone else to get into trouble with or build a relationship with. I did not blame Chris for Drake's shortcomings, just like I do not blame Drake for Chris's. The boys were whatever state they were in not because of each other but because of themselves.

Chris liked being at the house, and I liked having him around. He would speak so much about his dreams, and I so desperately wanted to help him achieve them. Chris had a ton of dreams. He wanted to be successful, build a career in a trade, anything that worked with his hands, plumber or electrician. He wanted to have a family and be loved and valued.

It was okay at my house to be who and what you were—there wasn't a lot of judgment. But there were a lot of lectures on making good choices and doing what feels right.

I think my lectures were one of the things that Chris liked. Even though he would tease me about being "Lecture Lorri," he liked that I cared; he liked that I would take the time to talk to him; he liked that I was aware of his dreams, behaviours, and direction.

So, as much as I lectured, it made him feel like he was noticed, not invisible, uncared for, or unwanted. It made him feel loved and that always made my heart happy for him. I knew that I wouldn't replace the abandonment that he felt from both of his biological parents, or that fact that he felt he was not being good enough for his stepdad; however, I knew that it would give him a little hope and love that would hopefully help him feel better about himself—not the false fear-based ego that so many of us display in the world, but the real self-esteem soul self.

Chris and I had some pretty good heart-to-hearts, especially when we talked about his sister. Because his own mother was a heroin addict, he had a lot of things he wanted to provide for his sister and protect her from. He would like to protect her from their mother, hoping that he could conceal the worst parts of his mom for her. He wanted her to know she was loved and valued, the same things he wanted for himself. He had great intentions to take care of her. If she knew it or not, he truly loved her and wanted to protect her from as much as he could, mostly from the addiction their mother was in.

The thing was, he had such strong family values, and so desperately wanted to have his family, he unfortunately got swallowed up by his mother's addiction.

So not only did he have to protect his sister from his mother, he also had to protect his sister from himself. His mother got him hooked on heroin. She used with him. It was heart-breaking for me to watch Christopher spiral out of control. How his biological mother could do drugs with her son is beyond me. How you can watch your son just about die in front of you from a drug overdose and still choose to carry on using with him is something I do not even want to understand.

His mother used him for money to help with her addiction, and she took him down with her. Before he got lost in the world of addiction as well, he was working as a roofer; prior to that he was in sales. With his quick wit and charm, he was really good at sales. It was his desperate need for her love and approval that spiralled him further into addiction. He, much like her, like all addicts, gave up everything for one thing; all his dreams, desires, goals, family, and friends all given up to get high.

Despite all of this, I'm grateful for the time with Christopher and I hope that somewhere deep inside that soul of his he realizes I meant the words I so strongly use to tell him: "I love you much."

Of course, there was a connection between Christopher and Drake's arrest. On Saturday, July 27, 2013, after waiting and worrying and trying to get information all day, I finally got a little bit of news. I found out that Drake had been arrested for a serious crime, that he was in serious trouble, even though they couldn't tell me what he was being charged with. What they would say was that someone was seriously injured, and the charges depended on what the outcome was due to the injuries the person sustained.

One doesn't have to be a rocket scientist to figure out that they were telling me, how severe the charges would be depended on whether or not the injured person lived or not.

It hits you like a ton of bricks when you hear something like that.

How could this be? What happened? What was going on? This isn't my son's soul, this isn't the sweet side of him. I couldn't understand how this was possible. I know I sound like one of those people that can't see the forest through the trees, disillusioned when finally confronted about who my child was.

Except I was not one of those people. I have always been honest about my children, flaws and all. This was just bigger than I was prepared for—not that one is ever prepared for something like this; however, when your child is making poor choices, you create a lot of scenarios in your mind and think a lot about how you may react or feel about those situations or the trouble they can cause. It's like you are mentally preparing yourself for these scenarios.

They show up different in reality than they do in your mind. Most of the time they are not as dramatic or crazy as your mind takes you, but this, this was bigger than my reality, bigger than anything I could've imagined, and it was bigger than I was able to grasp at the moment. I would like to tell you that a lot of logic went into what I needed to navigate this situation, how to process it, what kind of self-care I had to do, and how to address the situation from all angles. But I would totally be lying.

I had no idea how to process what was happening. I shut down quickly, emotionally, mentally, and physically. I was down deep in a matter of seconds and what I mean by that is everything drained from inside of me. It was like one moment I had blood rushing through my veins, vibrant, alive, and in seconds I was cold, disconnected, hollow, and empty like the life force had left my body.

I knew in this moment that if I was unable to deal with myself there was no way I was going to be able to deal with anyone else. I think to self-preserve you start to address things little by little. You start to take what you know and chew on it one tiny bite at a time, and with each bite you analyze what do I need to do.

You know that you still need to function. So you have to try to not overthink. You know you need to be present for your child, the one they are investigating, the one they are looking for, and the ones that will be pained by their choices. You know you have to be strong but for what you don't know. For whatever awaits you, what you don't know is far too much. The uncertainty when your child is first arrested, while they perform the investigation, is one of its biggest hurdles. The not knowing is the worst.

The only things I did know, was that the authorities were also looking for Christopher, and Drake was in custody, even though I didn't know the severity of what was going on at first.

So, you just have to do your best to keep your shit together. It sounds like a simple task yet is one of the hardest to do. You're not even sure what your supposed to do with yourself. You don't sit down and have a cup of coffee or a drink. You don't call a friend to have a convo. You take it second by second, breathe…okay breathe again…and again all the while trying to get the worst-case scenario out of your spinning head and turmoiled body. Things are not going to be the same no matter what. That is all you know.

There are no concrete answers at this moment because you don't know the charges, you don't know the situation, you have no idea what's to come—you basically shut everything else down so that you can get through whatever next moment that comes.

I cancelled some plans I'd had for the Saturday night and spent my time trying to unravel what happened to place Drake in custody and Christopher on the run. I started with phone calls and found out that a few people had been injured, and one in particular was in bad shape. He was in surgery and it wasn't looking good. The walls really started to crumble then—not just for my family, for this person's family, too.

You don't really have time to process too much because everything is so vague. The world seems to close in around you, like you're in some sort of vortex. Everything moves quickly and slowly at the same time, everything is loud and quiet; you want comfort and yet you don't want anyone around.

The vortex is like a black swirling hole, and you are stuck in the middle of it, unable to move as everything gets swirled around you, pushed and pulled in all directions like a strong force beating you around and you're stuck in this one spot. It's coming at you it all directions and leaves you somewhat paralyzed, in black spiralling darkness with what feels like no light in sight. The reality that my son had injured another person and that the person was fighting for his life was a complete overwhelm for me.

You want to break down and cry, you want to scream and yell, you want to freak out and destroy stuff because there is so much sad energy running in your system, and you have no idea how to get it out, how to deal with it, how to process, what to do, who to talk to, and all in the same moment you want to go and rescue your child, and that means you have to be okay.

You have to shut down your mind, whatever you believe to be right and wrong; you can't process too much because you have to show up, meaning you can't let the thoughts consume you or try to figure out any of it because otherwise you will not be able to function. You have to be able to show up to love and support your child, in a time when love and support seem difficult. But how do you show love and support to your child who has injured another so badly?

How do you overcome your own thoughts and beliefs about things? I remember when they were going to execute serial killer Ted Bundy, hearing his mom's voice on television and she was crying and talking about her son lovingly...I remember thinking what is wrong with you lady, your son is a murderer....

This moment came slamming back into my mind and it became very clear to me; while my son wasn't out hunting people and killing them, the situation was such that someone was fighting for their life, and if the person didn't make it, my son would be a murderer. And in that moment, I understood that what allows you to get through, what allows you to keep going, to push all else to the sidelines, to show love and support is the unconditional love you have for your child.

Please don't get me wrong, I struggled with many things in this situation. I struggled with the fact that someone was so injured. I hurt for the victim, for the family, for the people that had to transport the victim to the hospital, the doctors, for my own family, everyone involved. I struggled with what could have occurred for this to be our current life situation. I didn't know what happened and I did my complete best to not create a story or picture in my mind to justify why we were here.

I needed information. I needed facts. I needed to know more.

I thought the best way to fill in some of the gaps was to reach out to Chris's stepdad and see if he had any information to share. In fact he did. So my husband Jason and I drove up to see him. While we were there, the serious crime investigator showed up, he was none too happy to see us there. The investigators would prefer we didn't communicate. I can only assume it's so we don't create a story if we happen to be harbouring a fugitive. We weren't, however, sitting around waiting for them to decide to give me scraps of information when the boys were in trouble; it wasn't working well for me. Staying home crying, worrying, and wondering what was happening did not feel like the best use of my time, nor would it have been possible. My mind would not allow it.

Once at Slim's, Chris's stepdad's, what I found out was that the fellow in surgery had been stabbed, and from the words coming out of Slim's mouth, apparently, my son did it. What the fuck?

I learned that there had been an altercation between my two boys and some others. That Drake had talked Christopher into leaving the situation, and once they started walking away, three other men came along to restart the altercation, which escalated into a fight. With the two previous boys joining back in. At some point through the five on two, Drake pulled out a knife, and from there it all went sideways.

Slim was one of those people who wanted to justify his

child's actions. He tried hard to contain his anger toward Drake in this moment; however, he was struggling. I know he loved and cared about Drake, though for him it was easier to blame than to believe that Chris was any part at fault. He insisted that Chris was on the run due to Drake's behaviour. Thankfully, knowing both of the boys like I do, I already knew it wasn't as cut and dry as he seemed to think. If Chris was so innocent, then why was he on the run? Not that I wanted both boys involved; I didn't want either involved. However, I wasn't going to pretend that one was better than the other, or that one was more likely to deserve being arrested than the other one.

Talk about a heart-stopper. I wish I had the perfect words to express how it feels when you hear something like that, as I mentioned earlier it was a complete WTF. I think your mind starts to swirl with complete disbelief as you reflect on how. How is this possible?

That was my baby, who I loved, who I had nurtured and taken care of. He was the same boy who loved animals, helped the elderly, and joined wheelchair basketball so he could still play with his buddy.

How does my kind-hearted son, who shows so much love, stab someone? Possibly destroy another life? As my conflicted heavy heart restarted, the severity of what was happening washed over me.

It goes so much deeper than words and for so many people. My heart was heavy and it certainly wasn't for me alone. You have some pain for you; however, the mass majority of it goes to your child in trouble and the ones you have to tell. The sisters, the dads, the grandparents, for all other family members and then for the victim's family…the victim.

You don't have time to wallow in self-pity, you don't have time to really think, or feel about everything fully, you have to be a parent and tend to your children's needs first. Don't worry, the neglect of your own emotions will catch up with you. You will have your time to feel. Great pain will come and consume you…it might not happen in the beginning when the first bomb goes off, or time spent in court, or when you see them in prison, or while on probation; for myself it was when I had pushed the pain away for so long, busy defending, protecting, surviving and the pain demanded my attention. It literally made me break into a sweat and have my first panic attack. It demanded me to feel, to breathe, and to no longer put them before me.

After our visit with Slim, I stopped in at work to tell my boss I needed a couple days off, that my sons were in some trouble, and I needed to be home for a few days. I have a government job that allows for family days; not that I believe I had the benefits yet, however, if you do it's good because under these circumstances, you're going to need them. I had no idea how much.

One of my coworkers asked if it had to do with the cigarette. I had no idea what she was talking about. She told me she had read in the paper that a man got stabbed asking for a cigarette, and something about someone's face getting slapped.

I know the boys well enough that if anyone got slapped, Chris was the slapper. Slapping was something Chris did when he was out of sorts. Drake didn't smoke cigarettes, so I knew he wouldn't be asking for one, and that it would've been Chris who did.

I figured that was the situation, but what the hell happened from there? In my mind, I was thinking how in the hell is a man having surgery apparently fighting for his life, my son is in custody, and Christopher is on the run over a cigarette.

I went looking for Chris, because I figured that would be the only way I could find out what had happened. But he wasn't at his stepfather's, and as far as I could tell he wasn't with any friends I knew about.

Christopher had the advantage of not getting picked up right away, so he could spin the story however he wanted. I didn't think Chris would better himself in the story because he didn't care about Drake but because he didn't want to go back to prison. He had gone to jail prior to this, federal, when he was 18. He would do what he had to do to self-preserve. I would expect nothing less; it's human nature.

I stopped at the home of a mutual friend of Drake and Chris. Just like Chris's stepfather, he was angry with Drake. Possibly because of the way Chris had already told his perception of the story or possibly, like myself, anger was easier than sadness. My heart couldn't take it. I stopped asking. It wasn't getting me closer to finding or helping Christopher. It wasn't helping me assemble the story. It was breaking my heart with having to possibly accept that what they were saying could be true.

With the walls closing in around me, breaths getting harder to take, and the darkness starting to consume me, I went to the salvation of my home where I could do my best to collect my thoughts and sort out what to do with my time, because the waiting was impossible.

I talked to Drake's dad, Mark, briefly to let him know that Drake was in some trouble. He told me that when I was able to talk to Drake not to cry, and that I had to stay strong for our son. It's funny that in this moment I would listen so intently to Mark's words, apparently hold them as almost gospel. I figured he would know what Drake needed, not because he had been around a ton or gave golden advice for a living, but because he had been down a road that Drake was on. He had made some choices with drug use, had been arrested, and dealt with the challenges of his choices, so I believed that he would know, far better than I, what someone in the same situation would need or want.

Talking to Mark helped me. It gave me the opportunity to let my guard down, to share my fears, concerns, disbelief and have a little bit of a cry. It allowed me to get grounded; it was what I needed to give me strength to carry on, to keep moving forward because honestly I had no idea how. I had never been in this current situation. I didn't have anyone that could really help me that I knew. No one I knew at this time had a child who'd been arrested for a serious crime, so there was no one to let me know whether what I was feeling was normal or not, who to turn to, or who to go to for advice or help. Shit, in my current mental state I am not sure I even knew where the front door was; everything is pretty turned upside down, inside out, and all kinds of messed up. Having the only other person who you know loves that child as much as you, to talk, to really share your sadness and fear was one of the best things Mark has done for me. I needed it like the air we breathe.

The serious crime investigator called me again, around 4 p.m. that Saturday, July 27. He asked me if I could talk to my son. He told me that he was hysterical and that they had not been able to calm him down, that they could not stop him from crying, that he was unable to talk because he was so emotionally out of control and because of this they haven't been able to find out what had happened. So they were wondering if I would mind talking to him? Suddenly they needed me!

Of course I wanted to talk to Drake. But at the same time, it irritated me. They couldn't tell me what was happening, they weren't going to even tell me they had him in custody, and I was unable to talk to him prior to this moment. But they needed me so they NOW let me talk to him.

It sucked to be treated essentially like a pawn. I knew they would be listening to our conversation; I knew that whatever was said would and could be used against him. However, my desire to talk to my son, hear his voice, to know he was okay, was all I wanted. So, my irritation and legal concerns went to the sidelines because my need to show up as a parent and tend to my child, even though he was 21, was still my top priority.

They had him in custody for less than 15 hours, though it felt like much longer. He was so hysterically upset they were unable to gather any information from him. They used me, knowing they could manipulate my emotional state, to see if it would help calm him down for their advantage.

Knowing your child is as safe as they possibly can be is so important to you that you are willing to overlook the manipulation by the police, or at least I was. I know it seems strange you wanting to keep your child safe even though you know in this circumstance, you cannot.

THREE

DRAKE'S STORY

So I agreed to talk to my son, and they patched Drake through. It was one of the toughest phone calls I have ever had. The line was silent for a few seconds, and then I could hear him, sobbing. While he was crying, he was also trying to tell me he was sorry. You know how that sounds, "I-I-I m-m-m sob, sob, SSSSoooo, ssssorry." Sob, sob, and then repeat. It was heartbreaking.

All I could think about were Mark's words: "You have to be strong, Lor. You can't cry." So silent tears fell down my cheeks so that he wouldn't know how broken I was, too.

I stood and rocked back and forth, like soothing a baby, which was in fact was myself, while I was on the phone, because I needed to stay grounded. I couldn't risk sitting down; I needed to feel solid on my feet. I couldn't let my voice falter; I couldn't let the tears be heard. I needed to perform one of the hardest acts of my parental duties I had ever had to do.

With a shattered heart, I dug deep. With the need to comfort my child overriding all else, including the fear of what was to come, I used the calmest, most gentle voice I could find.

And with it I said, "Son, they told me that you stabbed someone."

Within his cries he told me he would rather be dead than believe he stabbed someone. I made a mental note, knowing that whatever had occurred that led to this moment was too much for him to handle, either he had mentally blocked it out or he had blacked out. This may seem like non-important information; however, you are going to want to pay attention to these small and what seem like insignificant bits of information. Especially when someone is in such a vulnerable space.

So, then I said, "That's what I have been told, there was an altercation, and during it, you stabbed a man." I told him that the man was in surgery, and they didn't know if he was going to make it.

My son cried more. We could wear our denial shield no longer. The spoken word, the reality of this circumstance could no longer be denied. That was when it really came crashing down around the both of us.

My son was crying for many reasons; for what had been done and what was yet to come. He cried not only for the pain he had inflicted physically, but for the emotional pain that he knew he was creating for all of us.

I chose to not talk more about the situation, I didn't want to talk more about it at that point because I knew that he needed legal advice and I knew that they were recording our conversation. I didn't want to put words in his mouth or create a picture. I wanted him to remember himself or share with someone who could at least assist him in whatever he needed help with.

One of the most important things for me in that moment was to make sure that my son knew that I loved him. Shitty behaviour and all, he was still loved. I didn't need to go back to the situation and beat him with it over and over, it was very apparent that my son was feeling deep remorse and struggling with all that was happening. This was not one of my opportunities to teach, it was being taught naturally. It wasn't an opportunity to toss out a lifeline (remorse lifeline) coaching moment, this was a lifeline that resembled unconditional love. A time where he himself felt completely unlovable, I would hold space and love him. No lecture, just presence.

If he himself could not believe that he behaved this way, was in this current situation, let alone fathom that someone was struggling for life because of it, there was nothing more that needed to be said about it. Not right now, maybe not ever.

I shifted gears from sorrow to survival. I'm not sure if it was the shock easing up, the fact that he was still crying, the sound of his voice and disbelief and sorrow I could hear. I can not tell you what exactly made me shift, parental instincts, survival I don't know but I moved on to what needed to be done next to help my boy. I then asked him, "Have you talked to a lawyer yet?"

"No," he said.

"Do you have one lined up?"

"No," he replied.

Because I had shifted quickly, it took a moment for my emotions to catch up to the logical aspect of things. I slowed down, I took a breath and with all the love I had, I told my son, "I love you infinity." I know they are just words, however, I had hoped that he could hear it and feel it. He cried but it calmed him down.

I knew he was listening, so I tried to convey what I could so he would know that he was loved. "I wish I could come and save you, son; I wish I could come down there and make it all better, unfortunately I cannot." With that acknowledgement of helplessness I felt my tattered heart shatter a bit more.

With the tears on edge, I dug in and with strength and determination, I proceeded to tell him, "What I can do for you, son, is call you a lawyer and get you set up that way. Other than that, there is really nothing I can do except let you know I love you and I am here for you. As much as I'd love to fix this, I cannot. You are going to have to make the best out of a really bad situation, son."

It was one of the first times in my life that I felt like I had had failed my child. It was one of the first times that I felt completely and utterly useless; and it was also one of the first times in my life where I hoped that my words were enough and that he was able to feel the love energetically. It was one of the first times that I realized a broken heart was a true thing, and one of the many times, I wished that the universe (God) would barter with me. I realize now that it wasn't up to me, there was no way I could have altered this outcome. The what ifs will make you crazy and they do not help you in any way. As a parent, you have already looked at every angle possible, you have already done a ton of adjustments and have given your children all that you have to offer. The one thing I strongly suggest is that you practice better self-care, more boundaries, learning about your behaviours, and heal your own childhood wounds. It might not stop that feeling of uselessness or heartache; however, you may move through the feeling like you failed or let your child down more quickly.

I remember doing that a few times while growing up, that

bartering. You know, when a boy doesn't like you who you really think you like, or when your parents split, a family pet dies, a friend has to move because of a parent's job, or when you yourself get a divorce, then you start bartering. You do it when your children hurt themselves or suffer their own heartaches of young love, you do it through any hurt, that reasoning, that bartering, but this time it was different, I was pleading. I was begging and I was crumpling in pain. You are so messed up you do anything no matter how immature to try to make it better.

That's what I was doing in my head, but aloud, I told Drake how much I loved him and that I was there for him. Once I told him that I loved him "infinity" and I reassured him a bit with that, at least he seemed a bit calmer, still crying but able to talk. Then the police ended our conversation. After all, it wasn't about helping him, it was about being able to get information from him.

The moment the call ended, my body couldn't hold me up anymore, I collapsed to the ground and sobbed. My husband was standing in the doorway watching me through the entire call, and so he came over, scooped me up and put me to bed. I cried, and cried, and cried some more. It was so hard to keep it together on the phone, to not cry, to not yell, to not react to his turmoil. It was hard to stay put and not race down to the cop shop and try to see him, hug him, get him out. As a parent, our job is to protect and keep safe, but at that point I was unable to do any of that.

Still, I had done my job; I stayed strong. I didn't show any signs of fear or sadness while on the phone; I had given my son the very false impression that I was okay, he was okay. That it was going to be a shitty journey, but it was all going to be ok. Though I had left this impression with Drake, I honestly didn't know if it was going to be. I didn't know if he, I, or the victim, or any of us were going to be okay. I knew nothing except for the love I had for my son in my heart, and the need to protect and keep him as safe as I possibly could.

This all occurred not even 24 hours after the arrest, so there is no other advice I even have to offer if for some God forsaken reason you ever find yourself in this situation. There is no set direction, there is nothing but trying to put one foot in front of the other. You just take each second as it comes; basically, you are trying to get to the next second without completely losing your mind in the chaos that has welcomed itself into your heart and soul.

Although I was utterly broken at that point, unfortunately, my job as a parent wasn't done. I still had to tell my daughter that her brother had been arrested and someone was fighting for his life. The thought of doing that made me cry even more. I had to tell Drake's dad, his grandparents, and it was all so heavy and emotionally crippling. I could barely grasp the concept of it all or process the situation, how the hell was I going to keep it together to tell family.

Telling family was difficult. I didn't have facts, I didn't know the charges, I didn't know much except that Drake was one of the suspects in a stabbing, and he was in trouble, how much depended on the survival of the victim and it wasn't good.

After Kaylee, Grandma Di—Mark's mom—was the toughest on my heart. It was not because she made it difficult but because it broke my heart to hear her cry. She was a hands-on grandma and spent a lot of time with my children. Every year she would take them to Rathtrevor Beach for a camping trip in the summer for two weeks.

Kaylee's first trip was when she was two, and Drake's the year after. They went faithfully every year from then on. It was a tradition before my kids came along, and it was something she did with her older grandchildren. She shared parenting with me while Mark was in his addiction, she helped me with taking care of the kids while I worked shift work, and would share Christmas with me.

She had already been through so much with her own children, and with other grandchildren, that it broke my heart to have to tell her about Drake. Dianne was a strong woman, and I had only seen her cry once, when my nephew passed away. To hear her cry now when I told her over the phone was another thing that rested so heavy on my heart. I wish

I had words to comfort her, but I had no comfort within myself, the truth of the matter was there was none to offer.

When my daughter Kaylee, then 23, got home from work, I told her that her brother was in trouble. That he was being held in the city cells and was waiting to be charged for a serious crime and that the victim was in surgery fighting for his life. Charges would depend on the outcome, from what I understood so far. I will remember telling my daughter until the day I die as clear as if it just happened. One never forgets watching their child's heart break right in front of their eyes. As she broke in front of me, I dug deep like when I talked with Drake, held back my tears, and told her that we needed to be strong and that everything was going to be okay.

It would be the first of many times that my daughter would cry about her brother. But I didn't allow Kaylee to express, feel, or share her thoughts and emotions about her brother then, not because I didn't want to hear, but because I was unable to deal with her heartache and mine at the same time.

First, I had to pick up some of my broken heart to assemble it to take care of her. I am sad to say it would be the second time in a very short time that I felt like I failed one of my children. I am not saying that for someone to tell me I did great under the circumstances or tell me that I did the best I could, blah, blah, blah; I did do the best I could; however, I see where I could have done better.

I see that in where we are today, and I knew back then I wanted to be better, I just didn't have the ability, skills, or know how. I was doing the best I could, with what little knowledge I had. There were no guidelines on how to be a good parent if and when your child goes to prison. There were no self-help books to tell me what to expect or feel, nothing to explain to me that my emotions were normal for the grief I was feeling. That I would be stuck in the cycle of grief for so long while the boys were incarcerated. Nothing to educate me that though I was in deep sorrow I may have a hard time processing it and be angry instead. That I may do that to self-preserve. Nothing to explain or educate that I would deny my emotions because I would always be advocating, defending, or explaining my boys. Nothing prepared me to handle my own emotions; there was definitely nothing to help me deal with the strong opinions, thoughts of others, or the cruelty. It was a total crapshoot.

At the time, I had no idea if what I was feeling was okay. Was I being selfish, was I being unrealistic? I wasn't the one going to prison, so did I have any right to feel as heartbroken, lost, and angry as I was feeling?

I had many people tell me I didn't. All the same, I can tell you I sure in the hell did, and so did Kaylee. It shames me to look back and see how shattered her tender heart was, how much she desperately needed some reassurance herself. She needed to know that she was valued and loved, that her emotions of anger and heartache all in one were alright to feel. It was okay to have moments where she was so mad at him that she could barely think about him, and that was alright. She needed to know it was okay to then turn around and miss him so much that you ached in every inch of your body and there was nothing that could take the discomfort away.

What really shames me is how invisible she must have felt. I was so lost in heartache that I was unable to see that I was the one making her feel that way. I simply wasn't able to be there for her or reassure her the way she needed or wanted to be.

I didn't share the news with every member of our family. I talked to Grandma Dianne, Kaylee, and Mark. The rest of the family knew that there was trouble, however, what specifically happened wasn't talked about. At least not by me, not then.

It was too much, I didn't want to keep telling the story, especially when I didn't have all the facts, I didn't know the charges, I didn't know the outcome, it felt like I didn't know much and what I did know I didn't want to. It was too fresh and overwhelming. I didn't want to keep reaffirming that my son was in a city jail cell, that Chris was on the run, that a man was fighting for his life, and that life as I once knew it was completely gone—all that remained was the fragments of dust from the world imploding around me.

Looking back, I wonder if could I have shared or done more for those that I had to speak with about what was happening. Could I have made it easier on them? Could I have been more patient? Empathetic? Supportive? The answer is no; actually, it's Hell No. I tried, I did my best to be gentle when I spoke to them, I dug deep and stayed calm without having break downs and possibly that is why I only talked to a few people because it was too damn hard to pretend to be in control, to find the energy to comfort anyone when there was no comfort within myself to give.

I was struggling to keep myself afloat. Trying to comfort or save anyone else while I was drowning was completely impossible and unrealistic. You are in complete shock and the grief that fills your body is unbearable. The only thing that I seemed to be able to do was remind myself to breathe, yep it burns like hell and a part of you wonders if gasping in that air is worth it, yet you remind yourself to breathe again. It hurts with every single breath and as much as I would like to tell you that it gets easier, it will not...not for a while... breathe...and breathe again.

I didn't have much interaction with my son's dad after our first initial conversation, not because I didn't want to, because he was unable. Mark and his brother Tony ended up in Regina prison not long after, he would not be able to show up to support Drake or myself.

Mark's story isn't really mine to tell. His parents split when he was young, both remarrying. His youth was turbulent to say the least, and I can see why he tried to escape through drugs and alcohol, which eventually led to heroin addiction. He and his brother were caught up in the same cycle of addiction, each at times getting clean and sober. This was not one of the times.

The long and short of it all was that Mark was not there to help me with Drake, and the little conversation we had in the beginning right after Drake's arrest, that was all I could hold onto for guidance from his end. Right or wrong, good or bad, it was the only input I had.

At this point, the overwhelm and grief were getting the better of me and what I wanted to do was crumple into the sea of pain that I was feeling. What I needed to do was to escape the heartache of my own home. It was becoming too real and with each talk I had to have it was more and more hard to find some comfort within my own skin. I needed to get out of the house and away from the cold that was filling up the space I lived in. I needed to find my own warmth and comfort and it was definitely not within these walls. It was all too much, too much news, too much phone calls, too much ache, it was all just too much.

So I did what comes natural for me when I am in a state of

discomfort, I called my cousin Deb. Her life is filled with daily challenges and chaos due to her job of being a paramedic, though with that it also brings a beautiful calmness about her. She has strong family values and is as solid as they come. It's not unusual for me to reach out to one of my cousins in times of crises or extreme joy. We spent so much time together growing up that we act more like siblings than as an extended family. We are a pretty tight knit, so it is not uncommon for me to reach out when life feels off kilter. I am not sure if everyone is blessed to have that kind of closeness; however, I am. And just as they are there for me with no questions asked, I am for them.

When I called, she told me she was heading to her parent's (my aunt and uncle) for Sunday dinner. In our typical fashion of understanding each other without words, knowing very well that I needed her, she invited me to join at my aunt's for Sunday dinner. This part I am always and ever grateful for. There was no "Let me check to see if mom has enough food," or "I am busy can we connect after," it was as simple as "Come join it seems like you may need us." And to be honest, if she had not invited me, I would have invited myself because I needed that stability of a family environment my aunt and uncle had always provided. My husband and I drove to my hometown, to my aunt and uncle's where we hung out and crashed Sunday-funday with family.

I can't really tell you all the details of being at my aunt and uncle's; I can't tell you what everyone talked about, what we ate, or how my aunt created more to accommodate the two extra people to her very full dinner table. I don't remember engaging in all conversation; I had moments where the tears where hard to hold back and I was pretty quiet, which is not the norm for me. Normally I bring the loud and inappropriate to the table; laugh at my own jokes because I think I'm hilarious. I'm the one that says the things people are thinking but do not say it. Yeah, I'm that family member, so it was very apparent with my quiet disposition that they knew something was terribly wrong and yet didn't pressure me; they didn't force me to talk when the tears formed in my eyes or when I had to walk away to gather myself. They didn't shame me for showing up bringing my dark cloud with me. They set the table for two more spots and moved around the space that I needed.

Although she knew, they all knew what was going on was big; we didn't talk about what was happening. They all knew that I needed support, they could tell that I was struggling and that I was coming feeling empty and hollow. They accepted me in my state of deep darkness, they knew in this moment I needed unconditional acceptance. They did what I had done for my son, stayed strong for me, and loved me while I was feeling unlovable.

They could see the heartbreak on my face and feel it in the energy that I brought to the home with me, but they loved me anyway. Imagine if you will, having a big family dinner: you have spent the day preparing and organizing to have an impromptu invite of two more people with little to no time to prepare. To then have the people arrive with the worst stinky smelling aura around one of them. The heavy darkness, the moment they walk in the air gets heavy and everyone has a harder time getting a breath. And yet they still accepted me, in a very safe space they just allowed me to be. I spent a lot of time growing up at my aunt and uncle's home. It sometimes feels like I spent more time at their home than I did my own. Possibly this is why I had the comfort of showing up; maybe they had loved me so much like one of their own that it just seemed like a normal natural thing to do.

My aunt was always cooking and creating great food, and she was and still is a 100 percent Suzy Homemaker. Good thing her name is actually Sue! So there was a comfort for me in simply being there. Not once from the time I arrived to join them to the time I left the house did I ever feel that I was not wanted, loved, cared for, or cherished. I cannot tell you how much I needed that or how much I appreciate the fact that they have always and will always love me in a way that makes me feel that I am the most precious thing in the world, even though I walk through the world feeling so very damaged.

My family didn't shame me; they allowed me to be in whatever moment I was in. I was pretty wound up, pacing a bit, not able to sit still for too long. I just needed to move about, they didn't get irritated with me; they just let me be. It doesn't always go this way; you will have some family at times say things with the best intentions, but you want to throat-punch them. Example: "You tried your best...HUH?" That one used to make my blood boil. I tried my best, like somehow my best wasn't good enough, like I was somehow solely responsible for my boys' decisions and where they were in their lives. You will have family that feels you're too emotional or are angry because of the effect your child is having on hurting your heart so much. They will say things to protect you, and again you want to throat-punch them. For example, things like, "You know he has always been difficult," or "I don't know why you're so upset, he is probably sitting there, inside the prison with his feet up watching TV, while you're here crying." It is hard to not react or defend and the worst part is you feel unsupported, you feel like you cannot share or feel because they say stupid shit that makes you feel even worse, or it makes you shut down your emotions because then you have to protect your child as well as yourself. It's hard to navigate through everyone's behaviours and thoughts when you are struggling with your own. It is very hard to not take everything said personal, even though you know that these people (your family) love you. Thankfully on this first day of dealing with my emotions I did not have to encounter any of this, thankfully I encountered love with no explanation needed.

I was anxious about the next day when I would be going to Drake's first court appearance since his arrest. Monday July 29, 2013, which seemed like forever, was actually only three days since my son was arrested and I was going to finally be able to see him. The picture I had created in my mind of seeing my son was something totally different than what it turned out to be. In my mind I would finally be able to hug him, talk to him, and really for my own eyes see he was ok and I was very much looking forward to that feel good feeling.

Sitting in the courtroom that day with Grandma Dianne, my daughter, and my husband, I sat so that I could see him the moment when he walked in. My heart was not prepared, but my emotions were kept in check, if only because Mark's words kept going through my head, "You can't cry, Lor."

My son came escorted in by a guard, cuffed at wrist and ankles, dressed in the same clothes he had on when he was arrested, crying so hard that the guard couldn't look at him, or look at us.

Drake seemed so young, so small to me, it was hard to believe he was newly 21 and this was where his birthday celebrations had brought us to. My heart broke a little more. When he looked at me, I didn't cry; I kept it together. I mouthed, "I love you," and he cried more. I let the tears fall silently down my cheek only when he walked out again.

I honestly can't tell you all that was said in the courtroom with the judge that day. I do know that they set a date for him to come back, so he had time to find counsel and meet with his lawyer before his next appearance.

I also remember the judge asking him if he had anything he would like to add. He cried more and through his sobs he told the judge he was very sorry. Then they took him away.

That was the first of many court appearances for Drake and myself.

Each time, he was in shackles and cuffs, his emotions raw; a young man facing the choices of his decisions in a state of disbelief that this was caused by his own behaviour.

I only got to see his face when he walked in; when he talked to the judge, I could see his side profile, and then I only saw the back of him shuffling out. It all happened pretty quickly, that first court appearance. He was behind plexiglass the whole time, so there was no hug, no talking, and in no way did it ease my troubled mind or saddened heart.

My mind had prepared me for a false reality, and any slight bit of joy I had about seeing my son that day walked out in shackles and cuffs.

FOUR

PRISON

They took my son to Wilkinson prison because he wasn't yet sentenced. He had to wait there for a trial date. Wilkinson is a provincial maximum-security prison, which is also classified as a holding prison.

Time spent there goes toward your time served while you wait for court dates, trials, and sentencing. It depends on the severity of a crime as to whether you get bail or not; but it also depends upon previous convictions. My son was already on probation for an incident where he broke a fellow's nose, and so he did not get the option of bail and went directly to prison to complete the time he would've spent on probation. Much like the game Monopoly, you go directly to jail, do not pass go, and do not collect $200.

Where he would end up after this would depend on the out-come of his sentencing. Even if they found him not guilty, he would have still gone to prison to finish up his probation.

Did where he was sent make a difference? Absolutely it did, not only did it impact the outcome of sentencing of time, it also impacted our time. How the visits would look, how often I would be able to visit, how close to home or how far away he would be. He could either get sentenced to federal or provincial prison. Sentencing of two years minus a day is provincial; federal is two years or over.

The type of prison and whether it is a maximum- or min-imum-security facility also makes a difference. Maximum security means no contact with visitors, and inmates are locked up more frequently. Minimum security is just that—more freedom for inmates. Visitors are able to sit across a table from you, rather than picking up a phone and talking through plexiglass.

My first visit at Wilkinson maximum-security prison was completely overwhelming. I walked from the sunshine up to a grey cold building that resembled a castle.

I asked the guard at the desk where to put my stuff, what can I bring in, am I able to leave money and clothes for my son?

She was, what I felt, condescending and rude in her response. She kept her head down, told me to put my stuff in the locker down the way, tossing her hand in the direction I needed to go, and that I would need to have change to lock the locker. I then asked "What do I do with drop-offs of items and money, do I put them in the locker or leave them with you?" Not sure what I was interrupting, she looked up with disgust and anger and firmly told me what I could bring in with me, what I had to drop off afterward, and that they don't accept money for the canteen unless I let them know ahead of time. She would see about letting it go today but next time be better prepared. That final statement was too much. Here I am in a creepy, cold, old building that smells like stale disinfected not-as-clean-as-a-hospital not-as-smelly-as-a-gym. It did, however, have that same effect on you as you walked in the doors like walking into a hospital, you know where your stomach turns and you feel like you need to get sick. The waiting room was small; it was at the entrance of the depressing place you walked into where it felt like your soul died a little when you walked through the doors. It really was too much for an already overwhelmed mom.

Me being me, in a shaky, ready to cry voice as overwhelm consumed me, I said, "I don't know why you're talking to me like that, I don't know the prison rules. I've never been here before. This is my first time doing this. I didn't do anything wrong so why are you being so aggressive and angry toward me. I'm just one of the people coming to visit one of the people keeping you employed."

I cried. She felt bad, I believe, because that was our one and only rough patch. After that, she knew my routine; she chatted with me when I came to visit and was waiting to see my sons. She knew which boys were mine, and when I was doing back-to-back visits, she would say, "See you after lunch." She would tell me about the lack of parents that show, talk about statistics of inmates with mental health. In retrospect, she had probably become so used to talking in a certain tone with inmates that she hadn't realized how harsh she spoke to those not in the system.

There were things that I learned over time that I didn't know when I came that first time. Things like wear easy slip on and off shoes, and don't wear belts—they just make everything harder and take longer. I learned that you are not allowed to bring anything in with you. The prison had lockers for you to put your own purse/wallet, jacket, as well as the white shirts, socks, and any other allowed clothing you might have brought for the inmate you're visiting.

I learned that you have to let the prison know ahead of time if you are going to be dropping off clothing, books, and then only things that are approved are allowed in, as well as if you are putting money into the inmate's canteen account. You have to come a half-hour early and check in with the desk so they can get the inmate ready to be brought in, and you have to book your visit in advance.

The prisons where I went to visit Drake and Christopher had visitation on certain days, and you need to be aware of that, too.

The first visit was super-tough, though none of them were great. You have to arrive a half-hour before visiting, or you will be locked out of the building and not be able to visit at all. You put all your stuff in the locker, then you join visitors in a waiting room. You may notice a few things when you first sit, other moms or who you think might be a mom. I didn't see many. Mostly it's friends, girlfriends, the odd relative. You don't look around the room much; you pretty much sit with your head down. It's awkward, it's uncomfortable, and everyone is trying to pretend that hanging out to wait to go see an inmate is a totally natural, normal thing to do. It's not just you; no one makes eye contact with each other. That's not normal. We smile at strangers on the streets yet here in this place with so much emotion attached to the reason behind us being there we couldn't look at each other. A place where we knew most likely the pain in each other's hearts and yet not an ounce of support offered to one another. There we sat shamed and silent waiting trying to act like we were ok with it all.

You are feeling overwhelmed, embarrassed, ashamed, angry, and sad all in one big swoop. You want to break down and cry. I am sure some people do, and I may have, except that I believed that I had to dig deep and stay calm, pretend I was okay so as not to add any extra burden on my son's troubled heart. I never lost the sound of Mark's voice in my head, his words on the phone that time telling me I had to be strong and not cry. And I knew I had to focus on Drake's needs. I had to focus on his emotions, not my own. I make it sound like I did this for my son and in many ways, you do, however, I believe I did this also for my own survival. As long as I was focused on the boys, I did not have to deal with my own emotions, emotions I was unsure about and had no idea how to process.

When the prison is ready to start the visits, they line you up. Then you have to take off your shoes and any belts. You go through a metal detector while they are checking for drugs and weapons in your shoes. I never really knew exactly what they were looking for and I never asked.

Then you walk into another waiting room through some heavy doors. They have to buzz you through, because the doors are locked. You wait there until they tell you where you are going to go sit in order to see the person you're visiting.

Sometimes, you may be seated in an enclosed room by yourself and not in the set of seats in the bigger area with the rest of the inmates and their visitors. That happens when a person is in solitary or in protective custody. Solitary is the place they put a prisoner taken out of the general population, either because the inmate was unable to get along with others, cannot comply with the rules, or generally behaving like a jackass.

Protective custody is more for people who have molested children, beaten women, or hurt animals. Those prisoners are placed there for protection, because in the general population there is a standard of conduct, even in prison. If the inmate has broken that standard, then he will be in danger in the general population.

In solitary confinement or protective custody, the prisoners come in individually, separated from the other inmates. The door to the prison side is locked, and they get shut in their room. At Wilkinson, there were three of these separated box rooms for those types of inmates and situations. They are basically still keeping the inmate in protective custody or solitary while they have their visit.

If your inmate is in the general population, you enter a big room that has approximately 8 to 10 seats, like little workstations with plexiglass going all the way through and on each side. Some of the stations have two seats, in case two people go to visit the same inmate. There are phone handles like the top of an old rotary phone on the visitor's side. On the other side of the plexiglass it is the same, except that there is only one seat and one phone handle.

As the inmate reaches this area, the prison guard uncuffs the inmate and walks him to the station he will be sitting at. Because sometimes they have to walk past other inmates, the prison does its best to make sure there are no ongoing riffs between prisoners within that specific area. The entire space is for inmates who function within the general population of the prison.

Assuming your inmate is in that general population, as Drake and Christopher were, you enter the big room and sit down at one of the "workstations." Once everyone is in this room, the prison shuts the door behind you and it locks. You cannot leave again until the time is up. You stay there and you wait for your inmate.

No matter which area you are sitting in while you wait for your inmate to arrive, you always clean your plexiglass and phone handles and mouthpieces.

I found the differentiation between general population and protective custody to be a part of the prison system that was interesting. Each and every inmate has committed some sort of crime, broken the law someway to place themselves inside the prison walls and yet some of these crimes are more acceptable than others. Somehow, amongst the criminals they have developed a code within of what is acceptable and what is not—a hierarchy. What you did outside the prison to end up inside placed you within the hierarchy, and what you did inside also placed you within the hierarchy. I didn't want to know what went on behind those walls, just as I didn't want to know what happened to my son in there, or where his placement in that hierarchy was.

For anyone experiencing the situation of having a child in prison, it's important to figure out some coping skills and find some support for yourself. It may not be easy, but you will need. You will want something in place. You will need it, particularly for that time when you stop denying your heart the pain it feels, and it all comes busting apart more so than it already has. I suggest you get individual counselling, find a support group, write in a journal, just do what you need to do to be the best you can be, learn about your feelings and find an outlet to release some of the crazy energy that is vibrating throughout your body. Painting, yoga, dancing—anything that helps expel expression.

But for now, when you are seated in the long row of seats facing plexiglass, waiting for your prisoner to arrive, you are just trying to get through the visit. You try not to look at other inmates, no rubber necking allowed. You keep your eyes to yourself. If you don't, your inmate will be sure to advise you to do so.

You remind yourself that now you are here, you cannot leave until the visit time is up. Knowing that you cannot get out until they unlock the door is uncomfortable and leaves you feeling vulnerable and anxious. It struck me that I was only feeling this for about an hour, it allowed me to reflect on how they might feel inside the prison walls for years on end. I had an hour and when that door locked shut, I felt it. I felt afraid, scared, vulnerable, and completely uncomfortable and it was only an hour. Imagine that feeling for your inmate's term.

That first time, as I walked to my seat, I cried a little and had to pull it together before my son arrived. It was a bittersweet visit. I got to see my son, but I didn't love where I had to go to see him. I had this idea that I had formed from television that we were going to sit at a table, and that I would be able to hug him. That fantasy vanished quickly, just as my fantasy about his first court appearance had.

There is one of your babies, brought in cuffed-up much like the court room, shackles and handcuffs, then unlocked, walked to the seat in front of you. You alone can see the pale hollow look of his face and eyes, and only you can see the sadness he can't allow the other inmates to see.

All I wanted to do was give him a hug, protect him from himself and his choices; protect him from where he had ended up, but I could not. As that realization sets in, you ache a little bit more, just when you thought it wasn't possible to feel any more broken: you are. Every visit was as hard as the first. I understand why some people don't go for visits. The experience is like running into a brick wall at the fastest pace possible. You slam against it and then crumble to the ground. Your body feels broken. It hurts so badly, and you feel like you should never do it again.

Yet, you get up and you do it over and over and over. This was the first visit, and I knew for sure I had a few months to go of visits. At that point, I had no idea how long it would be after that. The only thing that changed was I had more to talk about in between visits. The first visit is all about adapting to the situation, the talk is small, you basically are in overwhelm, as was he. We didn't talk much about the hows, the whys, or what was to come next; it was a fragile adjustment for our hearts to adapt to our current situation while still holding on to love and hope.

I went back to work after the weekend, but I hadn't put a lot of thought into how it was going to look for me to be there. I was doing my best to process my emotions. With the situation being so public, in the paper, on the TV and radio news, I feel I did pretty good. Though at that point I do not think I realized how shattered my life was. I didn't realize how people's thoughts and opinions were going to affect me, let alone that people would have them. I didn't even consider that people would be talking about it in the lunchroom while I walk in, the warehouse without realizing I am there, or standing at the till listening to the gossip. Looking back, I am pretty sure I was still in shock and had not fully grasped the dynamics of my "new life."

It was hard enough trying to deal with my own thoughts as

well as my coworkers', to find myself standing at the till waiting to serve the public at my job, to have to hear them talk about the situation. To hear their thoughts and opinions, not only of my children, but of what kind of person they thought I was. To hear them project their own image to the case, to capture the picture of the monsters they had made us out to be. It was extremely hard to not react, specially being in such a vulnerable unhealthy mindset. To hear them talk about the accused (my children) being horrible people, how it must be because they came from a terrible home. Probably welfare family, not educated. So can you imagine what the mother must be like for them to turn out this way. It was hard to smile, to serve them and be kind when what I really wanted to do was be like, "Yep that's me. I'm the mom; I'm the horrible home, not on welfare, actually a government worker with an education. All me…what do you think of me now? Still want me to serve you?" It is a lesson I will never forget, when I realized how easy it was for us as a population to create a story in our minds, how we placed people into certain life circumstances to be addicts, criminals, horrible people. From what I could grasp from the chatter, my children were a direct response to me, I can tell you that isn't true. I only had an influence for a very short time period; the rest is up to them.

It was extremely hurtful for many reasons. One to have them put down someone that I love very much, that they don't know at all. It always hurts to hear anything negative about someone that you love and cherish; it becomes personal. For it to be formed from a single situation and for that to be what people will define my child as forever hurt my heart. To know who they are talking about differently than who and what they describe. For people to be so concrete in their thoughts and perceptions with little to no knowledge of anyone involved, except what was fed to them by media, saddened me. It was challenging because I had my own emotions that I was trying to deal with. I was always on the end of the defence side when I would hear the public talk shitty about my boys, even if I didn't say anything, my back was up. I was always in a protective mode, which didn't allow me to have time to process my own emotions and feelings. It was also embarrassing at times for many of the same reasons, people's comments mostly said in not knowing who I was or who they were talking about. If these people knew who they were talking to, if they knew I was the parent, they may not speak so openly and freely in the thoughts they had. Maybe they would. I have realized that some feel justified in what they think when it comes to criminals, no matter who it affects. Then do you bother to say anything with the risk of getting into a confrontation with a complete stranger trying to justify that you are a good mom, a good person, and even though your kids have made a bad decision they aren't all bad, they have good qualities as well! And then the anger sets in.

One of the toppers for me was when my coworkers complained to my boss about me not being happy at work, that I seemed to be in a bit of a mood all the time. They had some false expectation that I was to be happy, that somehow having my day-to-day life torn apart didn't equate into discomfort and pain. Somehow it was overlooked that with my boys in prison my life had been tossed completely upside down. That the extreme heartache, turmoil, and grief I was in was completely disregarded. To the point it wasn't talked about, questioned, or thought of. I would get the odd question about the situation, but most of the time it wasn't because they cared, it was to fuel the gossip chain.

I found myself in rooms filled with people and yet I felt very much alone. I am not surprised that I only lasted three weeks at work from the time of the arrest. I did try to go back to work a few times, however, while my sons were in prison so was a part of me, my heart—and it was impossible to break out of those bars.

I was stuck in one of the phases of the grief cycle and was unable to move through it. The grief cycle includes stages like shock, disbelief, denial, bargaining, guilt, depression, and then acceptance and hope. I was unable to process the next step because I was still locked up myself, in the beginning stages. I couldn't move forward, I couldn't move backward; I was unable to complete the process. With being unable to grieve properly, acceptance and hope seemed completely out of reach.

The employees at the stores where I worked were directed by the area manager to not talk to me about my sons. I didn't know this until later and I cannot tell you 100 percent on the whys; I will presume controversial possibilities of altercation and disruption within the workplace. Had I known prior, maybe my feelings toward my coworkers would have been different, though a part of me still believes if they genuinely cared they would have behaved different. Don't get me wrong, I would have been totally open to support—if someone was truly interested and cared about me, what I was going through, or how my boys were, I would have loved the conversation. Those would be totally different conversations all together, however, with the vacuum-sealed approval from the area manager, the silence left me feeling like no one really cared about me or what I was going through. It was as though I was isolated and what I was going through was dismissed, they were unable to process or understand that I was in a deep state of grief.

They didn't seem to care about my pain. Maybe they didn't think I deserved to have any because it was associated with a crime. Had the circumstances been different like a death or hospitalization of my child, I know they would not have been so quick to start putting my children down or talk so poorly about them.

I did my complete best to smile, to put on a happy face and be productive at work. To overlook the judgments and shaming to be an active member of the team. I can tell you it is not an easy task when you are feeling completely empty and broken. Over the course of the three weeks that I managed to show up for work, the incredible amount of pain I was carrying got the better of me. With each day the weight of my discomfort filled up more and more space within my body. Like a poison slowly coursing through your veins, spreading itself out to every muscle, tissue, organ, and living thing within you, slowly but surely snuffing out the life force inside you. The pain of missing my boys, my family life, the uncertainty of their fate, our future, and feeling like I was dying from the inside out, I wasn't sure how much longer I could keep going. I knew that my coping skills seemed to be shrinking rapidly with each day that passed, I left work on my birthday feeling more alone than I ever had before and wasn't sure I was able to keep going this way.

Over that three-week period from the time my son was arrested until I left work, I had a slew of emotions. I was in disbelief, shock, fear, sadness, anger, hopeful—I can't tell you in what order or if it was just on a repeat cycle. All I can tell you for sure is that I was all over the map. My emotions had no set reasoning it seemed. They were high, low, and they changed so rapidly it was hard to keep up. The only constant was this low vibration that I could feel burn my throat at times when I wanted to speak curtly to those who said things I found insulting, or the burn that would fill my tummy and I would want to vomit when they put my child down, or the burn that vibrated through my legs to my hips so they felt like they were on fire when I had to stand and listen to cruel words because it was my job and I could not afford to lose it or react toward customers and/or coworkers. I could feel this vibration become stronger and stronger as the weeks passed until it consumed me, the pain, the fire burning sensation making it impossible to sleep, move, concentrate, to be anything other than angry.

I knew it was time to leave work when at home I had a complete spaz on my sister while she was at my dining room table with my mom and her new alcoholic boyfriend. My sister was my tenant at the time and her boyfriend was spending a lot of time at the rental rent free and behaving poorly.

I couldn't handle listening to her trying to justify the behaviour issues, the threat he was imposing on all that lived in the home. My anger bubbled until I slammed my hands so hard on the table that it lifted, solid oak so you know it was hard because that is heavy. I scared them all, and I yelled at the top of my lungs: "GET OUT! GET THE FUCK OUT NOW!"

The rage I felt was incredible. It was as though it had consumed my whole body. All that burning that had been vibrating through my being was forcing its way out. My whole entire body was on fire—every ounce of me was shaking.

Even though I had slammed the table so hard and yelled so loud it was still coursing through me. I had to move from the table. I slammed the door to my room a few times, I yelled more at no one because they had left. I did that a few more times until after my enraged outburst, I sobbed with exhaustion. I hadn't felt anger like that before. At that point I knew I could no longer go to work or pretend everything was fine anymore. Everyone's timeframe is different for healing or acceptance. When we go through things that affect our heart, maybe our mind tells us that we ought to be okay, because we want to believe that we are, and because everyone thinks you should be.

It's extremely challenging to blunder through, and hard to know what's going to come at you, how it will affect you, and how deeply it can hurt. It is hard to understand how a song can come on the radio, and you are ready to break down. It's hard to understand how the room can be filled with people and you feel alone. It's hard to understand the anger you can feel when people question you about your emotions like you're not entitled to be sad, or when they talk behind your back. It just takes as long as it takes—it's different for everyone—to realize how broken you truly are.

Some people may choose to try to numb themselves, turn to a bottle, or maybe smoke a little more. I drank a little more wine than I normally would along with some very unhealthy eating habits, and I justified that as being better than turning to something harder or more destructive. In hindsight, it's all destructive, and no matter how you sliced it, I was using these things to escape, to not feel deprived, to feel not unhappy or unworthy, to try to fill the void that had taken place within me, to do anything to cover the pain, the loss, the complete upheaval of my old life.

And it did not work because as most of us know, alcohol is a depressant and overeating can make you out of shape and overweight. So, it's not the best idea to overconsume any of these things when you're already at a low. All that happens is you toss yourself into a worse cycle than you already are, sad, depressed then feeling shitty because you overate, or you drank too much, and then the cycle starts again with the added shame of self abuse of overeating or having too much wine. The hard thing is that you don't realize just how low you are, because you are just trying to make it through the day dealing with the low vibrating burn.

My advice is to find a healthier escape: Anything really that moves that extremely sad energy out of your system. Jog, walk, paint, draw, write, whack some golf balls, make bread or pasta, garden, anything and all things that allow you to release some emotions. I know making bread and pasta sound kinda weird, however, kneading the dough, same with pastry, is incredibly comforting. What I realized was I just needed an avenue to release and shift that deep, deep sadness because you can't ignore it, and if you let it sit there it will fester within your body and at some point unleash itself in a mass ball of rage. It will be better for you in the long run. And by all means, find yourself a counsellor to talk to. Just make sure you jive with that counsellor.

During the time before I found a counsellor and my sadness was running amok within my mind, body, and soul, I found everything hurtful and dismissive. I had a girlfriend ask me how I was going to celebrate my birthday. I told her I had no desire to celebrate. Her response was, "This too shall pass."

It pissed me off—this too shall pass, yeah, no shit; however, three weeks in was the wrong timing for me. It definitely did not make me feel better as I am sure was the intent. It felt like my friend was just one more person who was unable to see or understand my grief and was dismissing my feelings and heartache.

The truth was this: not many people could relate to my situation, and in fact I was having a hard time relating myself. If someone could have validated my feelings, one person let me just ache without having to justify why, and not dismiss my feelings solely because they were occurring after a crime and attached to the criminal, maybe I could've accepted the idea that "this too shall pass" a little better. I get it is said to indicate that it will get better, in that moment I could not see it. I could not feel it...and I definitely could not handle hearing it!

FIVE

INCHING MY WAY ON

A fter the rage outburst at home, the irritation to peoples' comments, even if they were said with a good intent, and my complete incapability of handling the balance of work and day-to-day life, I realized I needed help. I needed some tools (coping skills) to deal with my emotions, how I was reacting, and to understand what was happening within me, so I made a counselling appointment. I would love to tell you that my appointment was great, and I got the tools that I had requested, but that would be a lie. Unfortunately, my first attempt at getting a counsellor was not that successful. She cared more about the juice of the story. She wanted to know all about the boys, the criminal act, the outcome of the victim. I would try to explain about my anger, my reaction to people, and how I wanted to spaz, and she would dismiss it and bring it back to what happened on the night that life changed so dramatically. I would again say I need some help on how to deal with these feelings—do you have any tools or suggestions to move through this or assist me? She would tell me we would get to it. My hour was up, and I had spent the time filling up her story with details she wanted that had nothing to do with helping me. I left with no tools, feeling overlooked and unheard, with more anger and frustration than when I went in. It's a bit challenging, to be honest, enraging in your already fragile crazy state to have to go through the story, leave with nothing, fire that person to find another person, and go through the story again. It felt like work, and in the state you're in you kinda do not want to do more work. Everything is an effort, and my only driving force was that I was acutely aware of how very fucking angry I was, and I needed to figure out what to do with that. The interesting part for me was also learning that within that rage I seemed to have found some boundaries. When she had phoned that she needed answers on why I fired her, I did not waste my time coddling her ego; I simply did not have the capacity to give her validation for a job she didn't do, which was completely obvious to me that she had missed the point when she was phoning, needing me to care for her bruised ego while I was in turmoil, and I still needed help.

So I hung up and called another counsellor.

Our first appointment, I told the story, where I was at, and how I had lost it, my anger, irritation. He didn't give me all the tools I needed immediately, however, in the first appointment he allowed me to be in whatever state I showed up in and be okay. I shared with him how the doctor thought that I was depressed and might want to consider medication. He looked at me with such compassion.

He told me that maybe I was a bit depressed—how could I not be; however, it sounded to him more like I was grieving. He told me that grief was a funny thing and that most people don't understand it. That as strong as I was trying to be it was 100 percent okay that I was grieving.

With that, I cried and cried; it was like someone could finally see my pain and it was acceptable that I felt it. I would love to tell you that I was all good from this point on, but it doesn't work like that. I had a long journey ahead of me, years of it.

Like anytime someone is grieving, special occasions are hard. I was supposed to be celebrating my birthday and I had no joy; it just didn't feel right. Thanksgiving was blah…Christmas, that was hard. I couldn't do stockings the first year. It wasn't right; stockings were our favourite things at Christmas. I couldn't put them out; I did laundry baskets instead and filled them with little presents like you would a stocking. Odd I know; however, it was easier than having stockings out and some missing.

I remember not being able to sleep and listening to Christmas music; when Freddie Mercury came on singing "Thank God It's Christmas," I sang it loud and proud. I love that song.

Freddie and I sounded pretty good, but mid-song, the tears just started coming and they didn't stop, not for a while. I called in to take the day off work; along with many days. I know, my attendance at work was the worst it had ever been. Everything was a struggle, work itself, the public, getting up, breathing, looking in the mirror, life.

My day-to-day life was disconnected. What was a normal routine was lacking something each and every day, no matter what I did. I imagine it's like having the same job for 20-plus years, driving the same way to do the same thing and then all of a sudden, bam no job. You would get up and drive and end up driving to the job because you've done it for so many years, you're conditioned to it, it's something you do without thinking about it, a daily routine that is no more. It's tough to adapt, though mine wasn't a job, mine was talking to my child, hugging daily, or saying I love you infinity or much.

Besides all the heartache, you end up dealing with shitty people. Everyone has a point of view, thought, or opinion. Some put it on network news, Facebook, some say things to your face, some unknowingly say shitty things to your face because they don't know who you are. The ones I found most insensitive were the ones that talked to my daughter.

They'd say how we would be better off if her brother wasn't alive, they'd tell her what a bad person they thought he was. She came home in tears many times.

I had some adult friends—or so I thought at the time—say awful things to me, but none as harsh as that. She bore the worst of it. Shame, embarrassment, and more just kept building for my daughter. She very much loves her brother; however, you can still see the hurt she carries to this day from the backlash caused by his choices.

I know that he didn't intend for us to have so much pain or experience the blowback from his choices. Does anyone when they do anything? Humans are programmed to be a bit self- centred, not so we can be selfish, though it does end up that way a lot. We function in our day-to-day lives without the thought of how what we do is going to affect anyone else; we are busy getting by.

Run a yellow light because we are in a rush, cut the corner to save some time, drive home after a dinner party when we have had a glass of wine or a beer because it's only one. You say none of those things are the same as stabbing someone, and you're correct. It's not a direct action; however, you cut the corner and maybe it's too close, and you end up hitting a person you didn't notice standing there. Maybe you run the light and you hit another car; or you feel totally fine from your dinner-party drinks, and you end up in an accident and it kills your passenger.

Not only have you created a backlash for yourself and your family, but for others as well. I can tell you everyone will have an opinion. You don't need anyone to tell you how bad this all is, believe me, you know. And it can happen to anyone, experiencing this kind of treatment.

It gets a bit harder to go out. You kind of feel like Medusa. Everyone wants to stare at you. They definitely do not want to make eye contact; you may turn them into stone.

You're the topic of conversation, the one they whisper about when you walk by. Then there is that part of you that doesn't want to go out because you start to worry about your own behaviour and how you will react if someone says something awful.

You can only handle so much on good days when your mind, soul, and emotions are healthy and happy. When you're heartbroken, depleted, and empty, it's best to not put yourself in a position that you don't have the capability to handle.

It took me a couple months, but I did get back out there to face the public. I had counselling and kept my circle extremely small, because I had learned that even some people that I had viewed as good friends, really just were not capable of being supportive during this stage of my life.

Because my sons had committed a crime, it was like there was no compassion for my feelings. I was supposed to get up each morning and not grieve for my loss, my pain, my sadness, my disruption, my shattered dreams. Apparently, it all becomes null and void when your heartache is attached to poor choices and bad behaviour. I've heard it before, the mentality that people have, if someone dies in a drinking and driving accident, like the death is deserved because the person made a bad decision. Or if someone gets raped, saying she was wearing a short skirt and deserved what she got; she was asking for it. How arrogant and self-righteous people can be when they have no clue. It wasn't as upfront as that, but the attitude was definitely like, "You do the crime, you do the time." And whether that applied to my sons or not, I did no crime, though I was very much feeling punished as though I had. I was not behind prison walls, yet my heart was very much doing time.

Christopher was picked up about a week after Drake. And he went through all the same arrest processes, ending up in the same place. The difference was that Christopher had been through the system before, and he knew what to do and how to go about getting the things that he needed.

He knew he was going to get arrested; he knew he couldn't be on the run, so for him it was more like a matter of time.

He had his shit together when he got picked up, knew to call a lawyer, had clean clothes, had days to process and be more grounded in the situation.

He knew what he needed and how to get it, There were not a lot of court appearances for Christopher, unlike Drake.

I remember when Christopher arrived at Wilky, I was on the phone with Drake, and for the first time I could hear something other than sorrow in his voice. He was yelling out, back and forth with someone. There was excitement in his voice; I could hear the hustle and noise of excitement around him from the other inmates. Annoyed at my son's outburst while on the phone, I asked Drake who he was yelling at and what was all the noise I could hear. With more yelling between them I could hear, "Oh my God, brother, you're here. I've missed you. I'm glad to see you! I'm glad you're safe kinda way." He told me the excitement within the jail was that a new inmate had just arrived. I was like wow, pretty happy for new people. He said, "It's Chris, Mom. They just brought in Chris." My other son. I, much like Drake, was excited to know Chris was somewhat safe all while my heart sank that he was also incarcerated.

Drake and I chatted a little longer while they did intake on Chris. Once Chris was cleared and they were going to move him into a cell, Drake wrapped up our conversation, eager to talk to Chris. I later learned that the cellmate they moved

Chris in with was, in fact, Drake. While the boys were incarcerated in the same facilities, they let Christopher and Drake remain cellmates.

With my boys both behind bars, my life consisted of prison visits and collect calls; depositing money into canteen accounts, dropping off shirts, socks, and underwear (always white), books, whatever was accepted. Letter writing, making up crossword puzzles, rap song lyrics, and whatever other creative way I could keep them engaged in outside life. My heart was stuck behind walls, prison walls, with no getting out. There was no relief to the pain, and I ached as much the last day as I did the first day.

I would drive down to Wilkinson, and looking back I can tell you that I should not have done so. My driving was fast, erratic, and my emotions totally unpredictable. I was always on edge, completely over the top about getting there on time, terrified about missing the visit. It wouldn't matter how much time I left myself. I never felt at ease driving for a visit, not at Wilky, not at Brandon, and not at Fraser. I could have hours and still each and every time my palms sweat, it was stress wrapped up with some anger and sadness. Every fucking time. I ought to have let someone else drive; however, if they drove and we missed the appointment; oof, that would be bad, so best that I drove, misdirected anger at myself was better than taking it out on others. I mean besides the people that happen to be on the road when I had to get to a visit. I am grateful that I never had an accident or totally lost my mind on the road. Though I am sure I was close. Please take my advice; find someone to drive you, learn to trust, use the time to get grounded, breathe, try to relax, find a bit of peace before you get there.

Once I had to go see Chris and I was late, just by seconds, and I couldn't get in. He had watched me arrive, run up, and miss the door; watched me cry. When he phoned, I told him I'd tried to see him, and he said he knew. He was so compassionate knowing how sad I was that I had missed the visit. My third time feeling of failing one of my children in such a short time span.

It was the one and only time that I ever missed a visit. It might be why I was so stressed driving to them; the saddest part is feeling like you have failed them, the disappointment for them, the letting them down; it is very stressful going to visit appointments. It might be different if they didn't know that you were coming, but they did, and it was something they looked so forward to.

When both Chris and Drake were in Wilkinson, I scheduled visits back-to-back. So, I would visit either Chris or Drake, then go out to my car for half an hour and then go back in to visit the other one.

Sometimes you would phone to book a visit, but they would tell you no, you couldn't. They would not tell you why. Sometimes the inmate would be getting moved, but they aren't allowed to tell you if that's the case. Sometimes you would have a visit booked and drive all the way there just to find out you can't go in. One of the things I found most difficult was having no control over what was going on. The no phone calls for a couple weeks, the not knowing how they were or what was happening, if they were okay.

You try not to think about too much, where they are, or what could be going on inside those walls. You really want your child to be safe, and how safe is he going to be in there?

You don't want to get too inside your mind and fill your mind with fear; you will drive yourself crazy. The anxiety and depression you're feeling will be 1,000 times worse if you give in to the fear.

You somehow have to dig deep and find ways to stay positive, and it is hard. Sometimes you will be successful, though the majority of the time you are not. Emotionally and mentally you're broken, and it doesn't take long for the physical part of you to get there as well. I believe that you can only handle so much, you have to process a tiny bit at a time, and you don't even know how you truly feel about the whole entirety of the situation. You are in survival mode, meaning your vision is very narrow, you can only see a tiny, tiny bit in front of you and it takes you basically moment to moment and that is as far as the focus can go because you're not capable of seeing any farther or the weight of it will crush you, as it is, this tiny bit you're able to deal with, is already making you physically ill. You feel physically unwell all the time; it doesn't go away.

Chris had already talked with his lawyer and was told to see if Drake would write a letter saying it was all his fault. Drake, in his vulnerable state, guilt-ridden and remorseful had no problem writing a letter taking ownership of it all, even though it wasn't all him. Without consulting his own legal advice, Drake very willingly out of love for his brother wrote a letter sealing his own fate.

I struggled a little with that, as did Drake's lawyer. Christopher's lawyer was quick to act, didn't waste any time reducing his sentencing, and Drake made that possible. Christopher was done with court appearances and sentencing about a week after he arrived at Wilky. Drake took longer to finish up in court and writing that note for Christopher didn't help him any.

They wanted six years for Drake. Chris got a year with probation. Chris knew the system and knew how to make it work for his benefit.

I was angry at the time; I couldn't understand why Chris

would allow Drake to take the fall for it all. Drake had a far better understanding of Chris's behaviour, found forgiveness in it, and was ok with doing the extra time. I love Christopher, he's still my boy, but I did struggle with his actions; I did get that Chris was trying to survive, and he had always had to function on his own. He couldn't let his guard down. He couldn't trust in the system or that we would really help him, even though he had been a part of the family for a long time. Chris was the first to get moved out of Wilky and to Brandon Lake, closer to home. He was moved to minimum security because he had proven that he could behave and comply. The system felt that he would be able to get along in a less secure prison, without causing problems. I then had to spread my visits to two different towns, which made visiting far more challenging and less often for each. Thankfully it was only for a few months then they were in the same prison again; until they weren't.

Drake was unable to be moved until his sentencing happened in November, and then he was able to be moved to Brandon Lake, as long as they felt safe to do so. Because it was a less secure facility, before they could come, they had to prove that they were able to behave. The thought of being able to visit without a phone and without plexiglass in between us, that I would finally be able to hug him after four-plus months, I could hardly wait.

I had been able to visit Christopher that way for months

and it was lovely, we would play cards, crib mostly and most of the time I would win, though he was getting pretty good at it. One night, they were doing a pizza dinner for inmates that were in school and because Chris was one of them, I was invited to celebrate his success. That night the bus was supposed to arrive from Wilkinson, which we hoped would have Drake on it.

I stood outside waiting, and because there weren't many people, the guard and I stood there talking. I asked if the bus had arrived from Wilkinson, she said she didn't know. Of course she knew, another one of those things that they are not allowed to tell you. She asked why I wanted to know. I told her that I had hoped my son was on it. She gave me a funny look and said well, who are you here to see...lol, she probably thought I was stalking the jail waiting for the bus. No doubt she was ready to call security. I then told her I was here to see my son and had another one arriving, fingers crossed; one of those moments where you hear yourself talk and think, fuck, is this really my life? Thankfully she was non-judgmental, or kept it very well hidden, and allowed me the space to talk about the boys for a bit until it was time to go inside.

Christopher was very excited when I went to see him; he couldn't wait and had to almost yell it out: "DRAKE'S HERE!" It was great news, and Chris was over the top with excitement. I was pretty happy and sad all in one swoop. I had to keep my emotions in check, as sad as I was that I wasn't going to see Drake when he was finally so close, I was here for Christopher, to celebrate in his success. It was important to me to make sure Chris got the recognition that he deserved. I could not let the weight of my emotions take away from Chris's joy. I know this sounds like a simple task. We do it daily as parents, celebrating children at different times, dividing our attention and tending to each child's needs. My time was already so limited, my moments so far between, the restrictions and constraints that at times the one little extra added thing of trying to separate emotions was a huge hurdle, some that I stumbled upon often. I will always remember Drake's arrival at Brandon Lake, it was a bittersweet celebration.

Just like Drake's arrival to Brandon Lake, I will also remember his departure. Drake's grandma got very sick and ended up passing while he was in prison. He was in town when she first fell ill, and the hope was he would be able to go to see her while he was in minimum security. Sometimes they let you out with a guard to say goodbye to a family member who is passing, so there was some hope. Though with his emotional struggles of his grandma being so sick, I am sure he had an attitude, so instead of the request being granted to go say goodbye to Grandma, they ended up shipping him to maximum-security prison in Vancouver.

It was tough. I had to phone the Fraser prison, and it was a weekend, so there was no one for me to talk to. They said to call the next day. Finally, on Sunday, I managed to talk to someone who got the priest there to call me. I was so mad; they knew that there was a death in the family, and that I was trying to notify an inmate. Yet, it took them three days to get back to me.

It was Mother's Day and I had to tell my son that his grand-mother had passed away on that day of all days. It sucked. It sucked for many reasons, obviously because I had to tell him Grandma passed and it was my first Mother's Day with the boys in prison.

Kaylee worked so hard to make the day special for me. She created a little family gathering for brunch, even though she was grief-stricken, just like myself. She knew I was broken and to the best of her ability, she desperately tried to repair the brokenness. I realize she tried to repair it not only for my heart, but for her own as well. Unfortunately, when Drake got arrested and she lost her brother, she also lost a little bit of her mom.

It wasn't intentional. I was so far down the rabbit hole that I don't even think that I was aware, but how could one be so broken and function normally? The answer is that you can't. So, for Kaylee, she had the grief of not having her brother, dealing with the assholes who said horrible things to her at work, plus that fact that her mother was around but not pres-ent. On top of all that, then her Grandma Di passed away. I look back and am totally amazed at how well my beautiful girl adapted to the craziness that was our life.

I can still see the effects it has had on her tender heart. However, I have never been so proud. She persevered. She educated herself and worked full time. She started as a health care assistant and graduated with an A from the Licensed Practical Nursing Course, which she paid for herself.

Kaylee has turned out so beautifully well, and as much as I would like to take credit for that, it is all her. I understand her career choices: she is a caretaker through and through.

When Drake was released from prison, he stood up at her HCA graduation and said something beautiful. It wasn't even so much what he'd said, as the fact that he was separated from society for so long, yet here he was speaking in front of a room full of people. Despite the challenge of this, it was his way of letting Kaylee know that he was proud of her; that he loved her, and he was sorry.

There were so many sacrifices that Kaylee ended up making due to her brother going to prison. I know he didn't intend to hurt her or break her heart. He probably to this day is completely unaware of how much she hurt with him going to jail. I cannot tell you the number of times she came home in tears after Drake was arrested.

I think about it, me being a grown woman and having such

a hard time in society, how much more difficult it must have been for a very young 23-year-old. So heartbreaking for her to have to go through all of that, and I am sure that she only shared a bit with me, because she already knew that I was in a bad place, and she didn't want to make it any worse.

I think the thing that kept her afloat was Grandma Di and Papa JC; unfortunately, Grandma wasn't around for it all. I think when Dianne passed, her whole world really crumpled. Kaylee also established some really great friendships while growing up, and those friends showed up, helped her dry tears, and even thought they couldn't understand it all, they held her up in times where I am sure she was unable to stand otherwise.

Our first visit to the prison together before Drake had his sentencing, she, like myself, was not prepared for the emotions that come along with it. For the most part she did alright, I am sure because I was with her, until they locked us in the final room for the visit. She was not okay then; like I mentioned earlier, there is something completely unsettling that leaves you feeling vulnerable and fearful when they lock you in. She cried and wanted to leave.

Drake wasn't there yet, and I told her she wasn't allowed to go. She cried more. I told her she had to get it together before her brother arrived in the room. I know I was a bit harsh and stern with my words, like I was disciplining a child. I was probably more *grrr* than I should have been; under the stress and the emotions, I am not sure I could have been any better. I knew how the dynamics were going to play out if Drake saw her crying. Not that I was an expert; I had only been one time before, but I knew my children well enough that I knew how the situation would play out. It would be a bad situation; Drake would see her crying, he would feel bad and get angry that she was hurting, and he could do nothing, she would get defensive because she would think he was mad at her not the situation, they would argue, and it would become worse. They would come and take Drake out of the visit, the inmates would see Drake's vulnerability, we would be stuck in a room at an empty booth, she would cry, and I would be angry…all bad. So I needed her to get it together and we would talk about it on the drive home, right now I just needed her to stop crying.

But possibly the saddest time for Kaylee, Drake, and honestly for everyone was when Grandma Di was no longer with us. Kaylee and I, among many others that loved Dianne, were with her when she passed and able to say our goodbyes. We wished Drake could've been there but not any more than he did, something he will regret for the rest of his life, I am sure.

Back when Drake had his first court appearance, Dianne was heading home afterward and ended up following the inmate van all the way out of town, until she had to turn to head to her home. She told me she honked and waved the whole time, just in case Drake could hear or see her.

After she died, Kaylee and I ended up following the hearse out until we had to turn off to head to our street. We both said this was like when Grandma followed Drake in the prison van, except we were saying a different kind of goodbye.

The time she followed the van was the last time she got to see Drake, so it was her final goodbye, just as Kaylee and I following the hearse was ours.

SIX

THE PAINFUL PROCESS OF SENTENCING

The waiting was one of the more challenging parts of everything that happened, and it seems like I was always waiting. Waiting to hear from either of the kids, waiting to go see them, waiting for updates, waiting for court dates, waiting for any updated information. I was always waiting, and it was challenging because nothing is in your control.

One time when Drake had called me from prison, I hadn't heard from him in a least a solid week, and I was extremely excited that I was going to finally hear his voice. I had been worried because we don't usually go that long without a phone visit. I later learned the reason was because they had been on lockdown, which means things were out of control at the prison, and in order for the authorities to gain some control again, the inmates are locked up with very little time out of the cells.

I had just finished listening to the very long-winded pre-recorded message about a call coming from the jail and accepting a collect call. Happily accepting it knowing I was going to talk to him, my concerns of not hearing from him finally coming to an end. I got to say hi, but in seconds he said he needed to go. I totally thought he was just teasing but then when I kept talking, he said, "I gotta go." I was upset; we'd just gotten on the phone. Being sad and angry I was like why, I just accepted.

But he said, "Mom, I have to go."

I wanted to argue, but he firmly said, "I love you. I gotta get off the phone."

I could hear another person in the background, and in a hot minute I was angry. I had this vision of some dude giving my son a hard time and hustling him off the phone. In my mind, I assumed that inmate bigger, tougher, of higher hierarchy in prison status, because Drake had to get off the phone. I was pissed and telling my husband so. Who did that guy think he was? Why was he giving my son a hard time?

I wanted to get in my car and drive to the prison and make sure my son was ok. My husband chuckled at me, not too much because he knew I was sensitive, he then smirked and said, "What are you going to go do, Lor, knock on the outside door and tell them to let you in, that you need to check on your son, that you want to make sure he is not getting bullied and that that inmate needs to learn some manners?"

Crazily so, that is exactly what I wanted to do, as ridiculous as it sounded, every fibre of my being wanted to go and protect my child. I could hear how crazy it sounded when my husband teased me. I was irritated and frustrated as I slowly started to accept the helplessness that was taking up its residence within me.

While I was waiting to hear from Drake, waiting for my life to resume, he was waiting inside cell walls for his sentencing.

While waiting, I learned a little bit about prison life from him. The meals, lack of nutritional value, the fact that there are no pillows on the beds because they could be used as a weapon, and the cost of canteen items. Canteen is like a prison store where an inmate can buy extra things: vitamins, pencils, crayons, extra food, chocolate bars, and such. I found it all interesting, disappointing, and sad.

They charge a ridiculous amount of money for canteen supplies; my understanding is it's because they believe that the inmates are drug lords or high-rolling criminals who can afford the cost. The reality is that most of the inmates are suffering from their mental health and addiction so there is none of this "rolling in dough." To buy a 12-pack of pencil crayons cost $35, triple the cost of what you could pay in a regular store, and even though you can buy it for less, you were not allowed to buy them and send them in.

One of the things that I found strange was that they knew most of the inmates had issues with mental health and/or addiction and it seemed like there was little to nothing done to help them along.

They get fed the worst food, restricted from medication even if they were diagnosed and on medication before they were incarcerated. They received little education on how to help themselves, no supplements to help with stress disorders either. They all ought to get vitamin D, B-complex, or even one-a-day vitamins for high-stress men, but they received none of these things. They also received little to no counselling, and what they did get seemed to me to be mostly religious based. I'm not saying religion is wrong; however, believing in God is not going to stop your brain from misfiring or lessen your anxiety.

You need tools, coping skills, counselling time, as well as possibly medication. They did have a drug and alcohol program in the prison, though I am not sure how effective it has been for the inmates in there. I believe if you work the program and believe you have an addiction issue, it can help you. I found that some of them did it to lessen the time, help them move to a different prison, less security, more freedom. My understanding was that some of the inmates believed the behaviour was from the use of drugs or alcohol and the education would stop there. The issues run so much deeper than that. The whys one starts to use in the first place, supplementing one addiction for another, self-esteem and self-worth, codependence, and insecurities. The main educational piece is not provided. Please do not get me wrong, I think having drug and alcohol counselling in the system is great, I wish they would do more. Psychologist, counselling, self-help stuff, courses, life skills. Understand the who's, whys, and what you are helps one understand triggers and behaviours. Once one is aware, it's pretty hard to pretend you don't know. Addiction is tough, and people have to want the change in order for it to happen, however mental health is not a power of wanting it to change in order for it to happen. Lots of times people are not even aware they are struggling with mental health. They have functioned within the discomfort for so long it's normal to them. They do not realize that the behaviour is aggressive, impulsive, erratic, or offside. The do not realize that it was mental health issues that landed them in jail, they blame it on the addiction. If they were to learn more about mental health, behaviour traits, and get help for it, it would be far more effective in rehabilitation. More functional in society.

I am not saying they need gourmet meals or to be treated like royalty. However, the part I think that gets missed is that these inmates come back into society. So why would our society as a whole not want them to be better? Otherwise, it just becomes a revolving door.

If we have them incarcerated for years, it would make sense to provide supplements, counselling, education, and self-care as a part of their sentence.

Prison life was intense for me to view up close, but then so were the dynamics of the courtroom. Drake had already been in prison awaiting sentencing for four months. There were a couple of things that were big news in my town, one was of course my son's situation, and another was the case of a young boy who had castrated a man who'd been molesting someone close to him. The courtroom was packed when these cases were presented.

When you have court appearances, you are not in a courtroom with just you, the judge, and lawyers. Anyone can come and sit in the courtroom. The first appearance, I was in such overwhelm, I didn't realize how big the courtroom was or who was there except for the people I knew because I was so focused on seeing Drake after a crazy weekend, focused on knowing he was ok. It was the next court appearance that I realized how many people were in the courtroom. The number of strange faces, newspapers, artists, parents, and suspects.

This moment is when you realize any issues you may have emotionally about what is going on. Any shame, guilt, or embarrassment, you will know now, and this will definitely heighten them.

We had many court appearances before sentencing eventually happened. It seemed like my son and the family of the other boy both always had court on the same day. I now realize that they have certain days scheduled for certain types of court, such as family, criminal, domestic. So understandable both being criminal we were scheduled same days.

The reason this other family stood out in my mind so much was the impact they had on the very first day that we shared court appearances. When I arrived at the courthouse it was extremely busy, media was outside and people were filling up the spaces in the hallway. I didn't know the family, I didn't know the story, and I hadn't heard the news yet; they were already seated by the time I arrived as were most of the other people in the courtroom, for court to start.

I didn't think to look at the scheduled appearance posted outside the courtroom door, to understand why the courtroom was so full. If my son was going to appear in person, I would have to see about a time slot; however, he was going to appear from prison on video, so I didn't look. I figured the police had been busy and a lot of criminals were making appearances this particular day. As I would learn in a few short moments, that was not the case.

In both of our cases, the person arrested appeared only by video, which is what they do if the inmate is not getting transferred from prison to the courthouse. They're not transported from where they are incarcerated if there are not enough inmates coming from the cells to deal with transport to the court. The court will also not provide transport if they feel that there's not going to be any sentencing taking place that day.

These video appearances happen before any other in-person appearances are conducted, and as it was both of our cases were via video, so our cases were up first; theirs first of all. Their son came on the video, and after the court announced charges, when sentencing would take place, the next court date, and the inmate left the screen. Suddenly the mass majority of the seated stood up and started to form a line, from two individuals sitting, to the door, down the hall of the courthouse and out the doors. I learned in that moment who the boy's parents were.

It seemed like the family's entire band had come to the first appearance to show support and let the parents know they were not alone. There was no judgment in the people's eyes; they did not look at the parents with shame and embarrassment. They stood tall and said something positive to the parents as they walked by, giving a hug, or pat on the back, and then falling in behind them, so they all walked out together as they left the courtroom. It was the most beautiful thing I had ever seen. It was the kind of experience I wish I had myself; that kind of uncompromising support for a shattered heart.

My son's video appearance was next. I stayed to see his face even though he couldn't see mine and hear when I would be going to the courthouse next. Then I walked out of the courthouse, alone. Maybe this lonely experience was more impactful to me because I was so alone in contrast to the large support group standing by the parents in the previous case.

In general, the court was always fuller when a case was going to be sentenced or if a trial was taking place. It wasn't often I would see someone I knew, unless they became a familiar face from the courtroom itself. During Drake's trial, I remember walking in and seeing someone I knew there in the busy courtroom. I was a little set back when I saw her, and I said hi. She asked me if it was my son undergoing trial.

I could see the remorse in her eyes when I said yes. She was supposed to be the artist who drew images for the court appearance for the paper. She backed out once she learned that the defendant was my son. They didn't send anyone in to take her place.

The day of Drake's court appearance for sentencing was a

very intense and emotional experience. Worried about your child's fate, dealing with your own emotions as well as those of your children, having the journalist and the news waiting outside the courthouse to catch you coming in or out. They were not set up when I arrived; however, they had managed to get set up out front by the time Drake's lawyer arrived, he told them he had no comment. When he saw me, he informed me they were out there, what he had said, and then told me it was up to me how I wanted to deal with the press.

I was angry when I found out they were there, that I was going to have to sneak in and out if I wanted to avoid publicising myself more than we already had been or while I decided whether I wanted to make a statement or not. It felt like an invasion of my own private pain, and exposure of my pain for the world to judge more so. I felt under pressure to decide, and in that moment I could not. It stressed me out more than I already was, so for now I couldn't think about it. I could really only handle one task at a time and the first task was to get into the courtroom to support my son. Months after Drake being arrested in July, to now November, we were finally going to find out his fate. That was the task at hand and the only one I could focus on. I knew the Crown Corporation, which the RCMP are a part of, wanted Drake sentenced to some period of time, but initially I had no idea how much.

It was only when I got into the courtroom that I learned the Crown wanted six years. Was it possible that my heart

shattered a little bit more as I repeated what they wanted…
six years …the idea of not seeing my son daily for six years
crushed me. How I did not break down, fall down, and weep
like the broken woman I felt at the thought, still surprises me.

The proceedings of the court sentencing were different than
what I thought they would be. The Crown sat at one table
and Drake and his lawyer at another. The Crown presented
its case, with the facts and story lines they had put together. They went through how they perceived the situation that
happened, step by step, piece by piece.

Everything that the Crown prosecutor would say the judge
repeated. Sometimes it was repeated exactly the same way
that the prosecutor said it, and other times not. I found it
to be somewhat irritating, because it felt like I was hearing
the same thing twice and being emotional and agitated, it
seemed like a time waster. Annoyed, I asked Drake's lawyer
on break why the judge did that. He told me that the judge
repeats the facts so that he is able to make a clear and unbi-
ased judgment. So when the notes are taken the facts are put
down, not the hypothetical theory.

That sparked something in me; I found it completely interesting, and it no longer was annoying. It wasn't something
that hadn't really crossed my mind before and they definitely don't do that on the TV shows, so I didn't even know it
was a thing, I paid a lot more attention to the way the court

proceeded after that. What Crown would say and what the judge would repeat.

For example, the prosecutor said that Drake stabbed the victim with a ten-inch knife, the judge then repeated saying, "The suspect is accused of stabbing the victim with a six-inch handle and four-inch blade knife."

It's all about the lawyers painting a picture for the courtroom and getting their version of the story to stick. So, what the judge repeats makes a difference. When you hear a man got stabbed with a ten-inch knife, what do you think? What do you picture?

Then to have the judge break that down to a six-inch handle and a four-inch blade, the picture is different, isn't it? I am not saying stabbing with either is good; however, a ten-inch blade is going to do a lot more damage than a four-inch one. Hearing the information presented correctly, your impression of the situation changes somewhat.

I liked that fact that the judge repeated the information back and then the Crown would agree and carry on. Or, if the judge had misinformation, the Crown would correct him, and he would repeat what was said accurately, and then they would move on.

There was something in that, something that shifted my energy around it; maybe it was a feeling of fairness and hope.

There was something restored in me about the justice system that I had been finding so initially cruel and unjust. I am sure it's due to past history of my own of being a victim of a crime; however, this seemed to help me see more of a bigger picture of the justice system.

Sentencing is an all-day process. We had to take a couple breaks, so as I said earlier if we had to leave, we had to sneak out the back door to avoid the press out front. I was still unsure of how to deal with the press, and with each break that I had to sneak out back, I found I got more and more frustrated. My privacy, my turmoil, and my discomfort were disregarded because my son was on trial. It felt a lot like when the police needed info from you, they have no problem bothering you, invading your space and time for what they need, kinda like the press, they do not care how you feel, how it comes out, or the effects it will have on you, just as long as they can sell it to the public. With those thoughts I just became more overwhelmed and madder that they were there.

But who was I really angry at? They were just doing a job.

Along with the overwhelm and anger I was feeling, I also went out the back door because I couldn't make up my mind on what I wanted to do with the press. I didn't know if I wanted to talk to them, would I just end up feeling scrutinized and defending my son or take the opportunity to apologize to the victim and his family, and then was that even my place to do so.

The girlfriend who had first told me about Drake's arrest and I had a falling out during the months between his arrest and this sentencing date. But nonetheless, she was there in the courtroom. We didn't talk, we didn't sit together; we barely acknowledged each other's presence. She was definitely not there to support me, she was there to support Drake and herself, I gather.

She also took it upon herself, while I was still trying to decide what I wanted to do with the press, to go outside and tell them, "The family has no comment."

It was one of those moments where you stand in disbelief and anger. My emotions were already so raw and right at the surface. It took every ounce I had to not lose my noodle. Who the fuck was she to cross that line? Who did she think she was to go and talk on my family's behalf? She wasn't even a part of our day-to-day world and hadn't been for months. She had no idea what we were feeling, thinking, or if we wanted to use this opportunity so say sorry or anything. It was very clear she was not there for me.

I didn't say anything right in that moment; my emotions were far too heightened and my anger too at the surface. Not because I felt like she stole my thunder, the opportunity to be on TV, or anything like that. It was because she could have possibly taken away an opportunity to show my son in a different light, a nicer picture than the one that had been blasted all over TV, social media, and such. It may have been nice to show empathy and care toward the victim and the family, maybe for people to see that we weren't monsters. I had been working so hard at keeping my emotions under control and feeling like she took an opportunity away for the better of my son, it was tough to stay contained. I knew I couldn't say anything then, I saved it for later when it would be about her boundary crossing, missed opportunities, and not about everything else going on.

I did as I had been doing for months, allowing the feelings to surface slightly then folding them up and tucking them away to sort through later. I had been working hard on not being reactive with the emotions, not because I wanted to be a toughie, but because I knew I didn't want to fall apart for my son or for my daughter. I was it, what they had for stability, reassurance, support, and advocacy; I couldn't be those things if I gave in to the emotions. They had to be put to the side to deal with at a safer time. Many people believed that I was strong. I remember one lady that I worked with saying, "It amazes me with all you're going through, you still smile and care for others."

Isn't that how it goes, though; caretakers always take care of others, and we never really want to feel our own sorrow and pain. It is too overwhelming. So instead, you joke and make light of a lot of things to conceal how you're feeling inside. In the courtroom, I didn't want to be a sobbing mess wrapped up in my own emotions, I wanted to be a representation of the image I had projected to him in our first conversation that everything was going to be alright, I wanted him to know that I was still his loving mom, that I was still showing up and able to support him. I was going to be that something stable and constant in his very mixed-up, toppled-over world.

If everything else were to crumble, I was still going to be standing there with love in my heart and compassion in my soul. It was the only gift I had, and always had, today wasn't going to take that away.

All the same, I still felt the jolt of shock when I found out the Crown wanted six years from my son's life. But I was sure that for the other family six years was not enough. Though the victim had survived, he was seriously injured and needed more than one surgery. I know firsthand being a victim of a crime myself, having multiple surgeries and years of emotional scars to deal with, that no matter what the assailant receives as punishment, it never feels like enough.

Clearly, under my own life experiences, it wasn't that I felt like my son had not done anything wrong, or he was being wrongfully accused or anything like that. It was just that the idea of *six years* still makes my stomach turn and my heart sink. I was on the opposite side of the spectrum from when I was a victim of a crime. Still, the mom in me felt like that is a lot of years. Thinking about all those years without my son in my day-to-day life felt heart wrenching. That my just 21-year-old and I would not interact daily until he was 27 crushed me.

I don't know how I didn't break down in the courtroom; I don't know how I processed it in my mind so that I did not sob or gasp for the air I desperately needed. His absence in my world for six years seemed unfathomable.

Just as I was trying to grasp the idea, the judge said, "Six years is a long time for a young man in a federal prison. I agree he will get six years, but not in the way you want it to look." He told the Crown counsel, "He will get two years minus a day for one charge, a year for the second charge, and he will do them concurrently, so that he will stay in provincial prison. He is of young mind and slight stature, and there he will have an opportunity to rebuild himself. Upon release he will do three years probation."

I was so relieved and grateful to hear the judges's words. He had much more to say; however, I was caught on the former words spoken. Holding on to the fact that he noticed how young and immature Drake was, that he felt Drake would be able to make better choices, and that his opportunity of rehabilitating himself would be more successful within the provincial system instead of the federal prison system.

I knew the sentencing he was giving was a blessing. I just

didn't understand how big a blessing it was at the time. I was truly amazed that a man who had the power to destroy also had the power to build.

Once the sentencing was handed down, I learned that in provincial prison most of the men there were in custody for less pre-calculated crimes than those placed in federal prison. Many are in provincial prison due to mental health and addiction issues, not pre-meditated murder, or sociopathic behaviour. Now I had hope. Hope that it wouldn't be as horrific in provincial prison as it would have been had he been placed in federal.

I can picture my son as clear as the day he was sentenced. I can see his pale gaunt face, I can see the pain and the sorrow in his eyes, I can see the shift of who he used to be to what he possibly would become.

What I saw the most then, and in my mind again now, is my child, my beautiful baby boy that I loved and nurtured to the best of my ability, brought to this point in his life. And with that image, my heart sank.

He seemed to accept the reality of his sentencing much better than I was, probably because he could see the cause and effect of his actions. What I could see was that small child I loved so much and still loved, as well as my own heartbreak.

Most of his journey from here on is really his story to tell.

Our journeys become very separate despite the fact that we were both essentially doing the same amount of time.

I cannot tell you what happened inside the walls of the prison for him, how he survived, or what he did to survive. I cannot tell you if he was scared or for how long he might've been afraid. I can't tell you if it was easy or hard. All I can tell you about is my time after sentencing.

Nothing prepares you for how you are going to feel, the craziness you're going to go through, and the amount of time you end up spending trying to make sense of it all. Remember, the day that Drake was sentenced he had already been in prison for just about four months. So, you'd think that my mind would've adjusted to the circumstances by then. It had not! I believe the reason for that is there is a part of you that hopes for change. Possibly the charges won't be what you're anticipating them to be, or maybe your inmate will be out sooner than you expect. So, until sentencing, even though it's a heavy burden on your heart, you still have a bit of hope, a little bit of sunshine that it's all going to shift somehow. When sentencing happens, that door gets slammed shut pretty darn hard and fast.

If you can imagine sitting in a dark room, completely empty, and in the far distance there is a little tiny bit of light, almost like a cracked door, and in the moment of hearing the sentencing, that cracked door is slammed closed, not just shut but SLAMMED. And once it is closed, you feel startled, frightened, cold, and alone, completely in the dark. You try to understand it all, you know the space you're in, you know everything and everyone that is around you, and yet it all feels very different in this newly closed up room. The emotions that are about to flood over you are not expected, shift rapidly, and are completely unpredictable; none of it makes any sense, so please stop trying.

I believe that all the conflicted emotions you are feeling are normal and completely understandable, and yet somehow the rest of the world is expecting you to be different. It was hard for people to understand my sadness, my grief, and on top of all that, shame and loneliness were added to the mix.

I thought maybe the lack of regard for the way I felt was because he was already in prison for a few months, and they expected me to be over it? Though the lack of care was there prior, so maybe they expected me to not feel sad because he had committed a crime and "deserved" whatever he got? Maybe they felt like I ought to have adapted by now? I could never fully understand the lack of care or effort in understanding my broken heart that I was shown. It was a bitter pill on top of an already toxic situation; it was a pill I would never swallow again or want anyone else to have to try too.

That day, when sentencing was done and my son was taken away, I was left with an emptiness that I had never experienced before. Although there were people all around in that courtroom, family, as well as Drake's lawyer, I felt completely alone, just like when a door slammed shut. I knew it in that moment, and that was exactly how it continued to be for me.

Over the years, with Chris beside him, life was better overall for Drake despite the amount of trouble they got into and the things they did. They would help each other be better at different times of their lives, building self-esteem and self-worth. In many cases, they even helped each other make better choices, they also at times got each other in bad situations and made poor choices.

The situation that landed them in prison, started off helping to make a good choice, walk away, however it didn't end well. Christopher started the altercation with the two men, wanting a cigarette, slapping the guy's face, and Drake convinced him to walk away. In that moment they were good; however, a much larger man and his two buddies decided to get involved after witnessing the face slap. Stating if he was so tough then he'd have no problem proving it. They were both very much involved now, with no good choices left. With the three men coming to fight (to defend, honour, or prove a point, regardless of the reason) along with the two prior that Chris had an altercation with coming to join in. With five on two, it became a bit of a clusterfuck to say the least. Once the guy knocked Chris down, Drake pulled out the knife to defend himself and everything went sideways. He ended up using that knife, a few cuts here and there on some, but the large man that came asking if they thought they were so tough suffered the worst repercussions of that knife coming out. The knife entering so far and so very close to a main artery, barely missing it. That knife going into his belly, slicing him down so badly that when it was pulled out, his intestines were falling out from inside of him. I wasn't there; however, I can imagine at that point in time no matter how drunk, high, or fucked up anyone was, that sobered them all up quickly. Not just Chris and Drake, the lot of them. The men that wanted to know how tough Chris and Drake thought they were, the two men that Chris had initially started the altercation with. They all would of in that moment, I would imagine the fear of what had just happened would, snap them back into reality. Obviously, it did, hence Chris and Drake fled the scene. The man bleeding out and holding his intestines. The friends in horror trying to help. The strangers uniting to fight now scurrying to avoid the involvement. For one minute, do not think that this could not be you. You could be any one of these people. The victim, the aggressor, the bystander getting innocently involved. It happens fast and in an instant, and please believe me when I tell you it can happen to anyone.

Drake and Chris had always had a bond. Their friendship

started at around age six or seven; once they were in eighth grade was when they became completely inseparable. They always had a kind of understanding between them, a knowing of each other that seemed to stretch beyond their chronological ages. I know it sounds kind of strange, but you hear people saying that they feel like they've known someone forever, or that they feel super comfortable around someone they just met, and that was these two.

Who knows, some say past-life experiences create relationships in the present life. For whatever reason, these bonds occur, and they sure did between these two boys. Perhaps it was due to their similarities in their stature, home life, the absence of their biological fathers, or similarities of their stepfathers. Maybe it was their learning disabilities, mental health issues, their self-esteem and self-worth issues. As I've said before, for whatever reason, Christopher became a permanent part of our family.

It seemed to me that they had found a male bonding with each other that felt solid. They finally had someone to stand beside them through thick and thin. They accepted each other, flaws and all, and were teaching each other to be men, because they felt they had no one else to show them.

They both dropped out of school, which was no surprise to me, although I was not a happy lady when I found out that Drake had taken a little leave from his current school and the principal said he wasn't welcome back. I had to enrol Drake into a different school, and it happened to be the same school Chris attended. Being together they tended to get into more trouble in school than when they were attending separate programs. They didn't do well with alcohol together either, but they used it.

When they were at the same school and in 10th grade, things started to spiral down. Both of them dropped out that year, and they started to party more. Christopher had an altercation that led to a conviction for assault as an adult and was sentenced to federal prison.

The sentencing was for over two years. When someone is sentenced to two years or more, they are automatically sent to a large federal prison, which is a much harsher environment than provincial prison, so I am led to believe. When he was let out after 18 months, he'd already learned a lot, and not the best things.

Among the things he learned was how to comply, to pretend to follow the rules, how to agree with you and seem like he was going to action through and yet not. He knew how to make you feel like you had won the conversation when in reality you had not. He became a yes ma'am, yes sir, kind of guy and made people believe what he said, even if he did not.

He learned some hard lessons about getting by that changed him. Yet when he was released, despite all that, he and Drake were right back to being like peas in a pod. I watched as their brotherhood ebbed and flowed, seeing changes—some good, some bad. There was nothing I could do to stop the growth of their friendship/brotherhood, and to be honest, there was nothing I wanted to do to prevent it.

There was very little difference between them when they reconnected. There was still deep love and respect about each other. They clearly missed hanging out and the bond they had built was just as strong as before Chris went to prison. The change was solely with inside Chris—he was more guarded, self-protective, and somewhat reserved. He trusted few and allowed only a few people in. Chris and Drake seemed to accept each other in whatever condition each brought to the table. They had their moments of frustration with each other; however, they seemed to understand each other better than I did.

Once Chris was out, unfortunately, the boys felt like they had to make up for lost time. It didn't start right the day of release; however, it did not take them long. They started going out to more parties, doing a lot more socializing, hooking up with the ladies, and trying more drugs. This behaviour accelerated up to the night of Drake's birthday when he was arrested.

Christopher went on the run that night. He was pissed off, and blamed Drake for everything because Drake was the one with the knife. If Drake hadn't had the knife, things wouldn't have gone as they had. But then, who knows how it would have looked or turned out. It's part of the boys' behaviours as well, Chris tends to blame others and society for his actions; Drake tends to take responsibility, for the most part, for himself. This is still true, of the boys, to this day.

That night, Chris didn't know what the charges were going to be; however, he knew that it was bad and he sure as hell didn't want to go back to prison. Please understand I am not calling Christopher out or putting him down, I love him, I'm describing his mechanism for survival.

Chris understood the game not only of prison on how to reduce your time. He understood how to behave, to jock for position, to hold your own, and importantly, how to make sure no one bothered you.

Once Chris was picked up and brought to Wilky, he helped his cellmate (Drake) with these tools of self-preservation and self-protection. They were better together in there than they were alone, I could hear the security of having one another in their voices on the phone or when I would see them in visits.

Along with the grief and loneliness I was feeling about both boys being incarcerated, I also struggled accepting how the sentencing was placed and the impact on the relationship between Christopher and Drake.

Drake felt shame for what had happened and it left him in a very vulnerable place. Chris allowed him to feel it, and actually played on it, you'll recall that he also got Drake to write a letter stating that he was responsible for the whole altercation the night of his birthday, which reduced Christopher's sentencing.

The end result of that letter was that Chris received a single year sentence, and Drake received that six-year sentence, which was broken down to two years minus a day for one charge, plus one year for the second charge, and three years in probation. He was allowed to serve his jail terms concurrently and then serve his probation.

As angry as I was that Chris had gotten Drake to write the letter accepting all the blame, and that Drake had done so, they were both totally fine with the situation. Drake felt that it was best for him to take the majority of the blame, since he was the one who had used the knife. He also wanted to protect Chris, because he had already done major time once in his life. Naturally, Chris was in agreement.

What always amazes me is that there was no anger, only agreement and understanding between them, with one looking after the other in prison. To this day, even with Christopher no longer present in our daily lives, Drake still has no anger over that situation.

It might appear I have painted Chris badly here, but that's

not my intent. Chris did many wonderful things inside and outside of prison. Their time spent in prison together he taught Drake how to write and to do his signature. I know people think I am exaggerating; however, it is 100 percent true. Drake, at 21 years of age, did not know how to write; he could print, but writing was not something he knew how to do. They had time and Christopher taught him. He helped Drake with reading, and they did a lot more writing so Drake's printing became better. He encouraged Drake to take art, get an education if he could while he was still in prison, take different programs, to use his time and the system to better himself. One of the most important things he did was he taught Drake how to survive while they were incarcerated.

Chris was out of prison before Drake, so he and I got to spend time together. We read our letters from Drake, and we talked about life and the directions we planned on going. Christopher and I have always had a pretty good relationship. We discussed his childhood, his relationships with his biological mom, his stepfather, and his sister. Along with his relationships, we discussed everything from education to friendship, and the perception we have of ourselves and others have of us.

While he'd been more honest and open about his feelings, dreams, and ideas when he was younger, before he was ever incarcerated, he still expressed himself to me. He had already been exposed to a different kind of lifestyle in his upbringing, so in a sense it gave him a feeling that he was different. He had the confidence to say the things he wanted to say to me, argue with me and try to prove me wrong sometimes. That might drive some people crazy, but I liked that he felt strong enough in his beliefs that he would fight for them. That is one way he and Drake were similar.

I like to take at least some credit for this part of all of my kids, even those that I didn't give birth to. It's obviously not genetics, but perhaps I encouraged this kind of thinking.

When he was younger and not partying, Chris held a lot of strong beliefs about business, careers, goals, and how he wanted to achieve success. Later, after being involved in the partying world, his beliefs centred more around things like making money quick, and certain personality traits to justify who he was becoming. The one thing that I have always found fascinating with people getting caught up in addiction is how quickly they become victims of circumstance, situations, and life itself.

It's not really about owning their actions anymore, instead everything becomes about how someone made them do this or someone made them do that or how it was because someone did this or that to them. Like blaming the way they were raised, or the lack of what society had to offer them. I could see Chris start to shift more so in this direction along with more activation with drugs and alcohol.

After he got out of prison for his role in the crime he and Drake were arrested for, Chris did his best to stay on a healthy path. He did in the beginning; however, he really struggled. Even so, a year or so later when Drake was released, Christopher focused on helping Drake adapt to the outside. He wasn't so caught up in his addiction that he wasn't able to show up for Drake. They were still there for each other.

Their relationship was still intact and just as fun, for them, as it had been when they were kids. They were as boisterous and outgoing as ever. It seemed to me that the time they served together in prison had brought them more bonded in brotherhood. It seemed like the experience had shifted the boundaries of the friendship. They had no more vulnerabilities; they had been exposed in all aspects being in prison and cellmates. You don't leave your cell to go to the washroom like in school or work; your washroom is in your cell. No door, no separate space, right there for your mate to see. Showering is an allotted time and shared space; no privacy there either. Along with all the exposure of things we take for granted on a daily basis, they also are vulnerable with emotions with who they share a cell. Sadness of missing your family, your girl, or just a shit day for choices made. Thankfully these two were brothers and loved each other. They had one another's back, but if not, the time served would have been very different. Due to the lack of boundaries within the walls of the prison, they definitely lack boundaries in the outside world.

It might have seemed pretty odd to a lot of people, the way they talked openly about everything, and I mean everything. Sometimes I would cover my ears and be like, guys I don't need to hear this. They didn't have the restraints between them, the ones that society places upon us as well as growing up does. The lack of knowledge of the behaviours that they displayed was of innocents and youth. As one small example, one day the three of us went to Costco together. Drake had an ice cream and Chris wanted a soda, and halfway through the ice cream, they were sharing it, like little kids; they didn't think twice about it, it was as normal as the sun coming up. There were many moments like sharing an ice cream cone, hugging each other publicly, or yelling out "Love ya, Bro." It tugged at my heart, because of the years they had just spent, the things they had been through. Somehow they managed to make it through, not being too messed up, and still able to have each other's back even with the lack of growth while they were incarcerated. Somehow, they managed to hang on to some innocence.

It didn't take too long for them to get functional into society; they got jobs and then found ladies. And that is where life changed between them. They had such a strong bond, they still do; however, it looks much different than it used to.

Drake met someone who had a child, and he took that beautiful little girl on as his own. Chris was Uncle Chris, and he was around tons at first, except when he was partying. Then, he didn't come around out of respect for Drake and the family he was creating. When Drake and his partner were expecting, he and Chris spent less time together. Drake being more focused on the growing family and Chris more on his addiction.

Unfortunately, Christopher's drug addiction had pulled him too far down the rabbit hole for Drake to feel safe having him around his family. One of the hardest decisions I have seen Drake make was to tell Chris that he had to be clean to be at his house and around both his children.

Because of that, Christopher never got to see his nephew be born or spend time with him. Chris has missed out on some pretty important times, including times that Drake could have used his love and support. Much like the birth of his son, he could have used his bro when his son underwent brain surgery. It was sad to watch how far away the addiction was taking him.

It's hard to know which way they will go when they get out of prison, there are no books to read that tell you how to set yourself up to support your newly released prisoner. To be honest, it is completely up to them. Like anything in life, you have to be aware of the problem, be willing to be accountable and responsible for your behaviour and want to change in order for change to happen. Once they have been in the system for a while, it is very common for them to end up back in it. Life is hard. If you think about it honestly and how many times you may have struggled in your lifetime, having coping skills and a nonreactive mind then think of someone who doesn't have those skills. It is understandable that they reoffend or relapse. It takes patience, kindness, empathy, and in the same moment, stern and strong boundaries to help them on the journey once out, if not for them, for yourself. How you choose to react to them when they make choices is your only teaching tool you have to share with them. To be an example, to stand strong. So my hope is you have done a lot of growth and self-work while they were incarcerated so you know your own triggers and character flaws. For myself I am 100 percent caretaker, put them before me always, tend to have codependent tendencies as well as seeking outside validation. I really had to work on that to be better for when they were released. I have been around addicts most of my life, so I was able to see signs or things that I found questionable in behaviours, alerting me that issues may be arising. Sometimes it can be little things, like lack of energy, irritable, isolating, always needing money, becoming less responsible and getting attitude issues. When they want to spend less and less time with you is also a good warning sign, though they are in deeper by that point. I am pretty present in my children's lives even as adults, so I could see things, shifts in personalities, behaviours. You don't want to believe that they will relapse or end up back inside the prison walls; however, it is possible it will happen, so you have to prepare yourself. Help them out as much as you can but accept that they make their own choices. You can talk with them, be open and honest about your concerns, if they are reactive it is usually a sign, they know they aren't making good choices and don't want to be called out on it. Or they don't want you to know and are angry you have figured it out. It is part of the shame that goes along with using.

Just last year, Christopher got arrested again for stealing a car, and while he was incarcerated, I finally heard from him again. He called and wrote to me.

I cried while reading his first letter that I received. Most of what he'd written made no sense; the writing was all crazy. He had big letters, small letters, scribbling; it was so crazy that I had a hard time even trying to make sense of what he was trying to say. It was heartbreaking to see how his mind was such a mess from the drugs that he'd been doing.

While he was incarcerated for the car theft, Chris tried to clean up, and he kept talking to Drake. Drake was so excited to have him back in his life that he picked Chris up from prison when he was released. Despite the great intentions Chris shared while he was away, they came to a screeching halt the day Drake drove him back to town. Chris said he had to make a quick stop. Drake complied, and then waited for him for almost an hour, but Chris never came back to the car. Drake told me that his heart sank with the reality that Chris had chosen drugs over him.

It's sad for me to see how much their lives have changed, and the great distance that's come between them. But sometimes I am grateful the distance is there. It is hard enough when one of them is making poor choices, but both at the same time is sometimes more than my heart can handle.

I often say that Mark, Drake's dad, conditioned me for these times with the boys. He gave me the insight of loving someone who has an addiction problem, how you can love someone or something; however, if you're an addict you love your addiction more. How powerless one can be over it. However, I did find it was a bit different going through it with the boys than with a spouse. We have expectations out of both children and spouses, except we don't feel as responsible for our spouses as we do our children. It was harder on my heart with the boys. Without the experience I had gone through with Mark, I might not have been able to understand what was going on with either Drake or Chris. I understand that not everyone is going to be able to have this sort of insight, and for that I am grateful that you haven't had to experience the heartache of an addict effecting your world. And for those of you that know what I am talking about, I am sorry for your ache.

SEVEN

COMING HOME

The night before you go to the prison to see your son there for the last time, to pick up the person you've been visiting all these years, something inside you shifts. It's a movement of energy that you haven't had in what seems like forever.

You still have that anxiousness you've felt for the last few years, you still feel edgy and somewhat agitated. The agitation has become your constant companion, after all. But now there is something else moving its way through your body, something that is forcing whatever it is you have been feeling for the last few years to move over, to create a little space for itself.

This new-formed energy finding its way into your body is joy. It was something that had not moved in me for the years that my son was incarcerated.

The night before I was to get Drake, I went over to Vancouver from home so I could be closer to the prison. They'd told me he would be released in the morning, and because of when the morning ferry ran, I would miss the release hour unless I stayed closer.

Staying in Vancouver felt strange. I was one step closer to never having to go to the prison ever again, but I still had to get through the night ahead. And even though he was scheduled to be released, there was no guarantee his release was going to happen. He could get into a fight with an inmate or any number of things could happen that would delay that release, from prison unrest to paperwork, all of them out of my control.

I got the closest hotel I could to the prison that I could find. After I checked in and settled down for the night, I still didn't get much sleep. I had so many feelings that were just rising to the surface and finding their way past the pain I'd been feeling non-stop for years.

How could I sleep when I was feeling all at once anxious, nervous, overwhelmed, happy, excited, worried, and I am not going to lie, a little afraid. I was going to the prison, and this time when I left, I was going to be able to bring my baby home. For the first time I was going to go and not leave him there, for the first time when I left the prison grounds, I would not feel like I needed to vomit, not feel like I was making the biggest mistake leaving someone I loved more than life itself in one of the most horrific places ever. It feels so wrong leaving your child there; it goes against everything in your entire being.

Going to the prison to bring Drake home felt similar to the excitement of bringing home a new baby, except with sorrow and fear attached.

I arrived at the prison early. I waited and I waited and I waited, pacing back and forth outside. Every time a door opened, or a movement happened, I was hoping it would be my son. I am pretty sure this was not a great time for my husband, because the longer I waited, the more anxious I became. After a couple of hours, I started to worry that he wasn't going to be let out. I started worrying what if something happened, what if they changed their minds about releasing him? Finally, in the midst of one of my "what if" rants, Drake walked out.

There he was. My boy was standing there. I wanted to run up and wrap my arms around him, I wanted to squeeze him for so long, to hold him in my arms forever. Although I did give him the biggest hug and cry a little, I didn't hold on forever. Not because I didn't want to, but I didn't want to overwhelm him. I knew that he had not had contact in that way for a

couple years, and that emotions were not displayed inside
the prison walls.

It didn't seem to matter to me that he was a prisoner being
released. He was my baby boy, and the joy that was taking
over because I could physically touch him, bring him with
me, talk to him without plexiglass between us, was wonderful. That he was standing in front of me with his freedom to
walk away. I beamed. It was like a part of me was recovered,
put back into place, a piece that had been missing.

Although I did not feel completely whole just yet, finally, in
that moment, I was able to relax with a full breath and feel
a little bit of peace. With that peace came some joy. I hadn't
been able to relax and feel any peace in a very long time. I
laugh a bit when I write this, because the peace that I felt
was the safety of having my son with me, like I was going to
finally be able to protect him. What made me laugh now, was
that I was unable to do that in the past, so I am not sure why
in my mind, that day, I thought I was going to be able to do
anything different.

I believe your mind will tell you whatever you want that allows you to keep moving forward. I was totally caught up in
my own emotions. Of course, I cared about what was going
on with Drake at that moment. We didn't talk about any
misgiving he might be feeling, in my excitement, I just assumed he was as happy as I was, to be going home. To be free.

I could see in his eyes that things had shifted, that they were not as bright as they had been. He seemed happy, and yet I could feel resistance and hesitation.

I discarded the off energy that I was picking up from him. I figured that it was probably overwhelm. From being told what he could and could not do every minute in prison to the idea of being able to make your own choices. I was so focused on picking him up that I didn't think about how it might be challenging for him to leave, the adjustment might be more difficult than just walking out doors. I learned much later that the hesitation was more because he too felt it wasn't real. It was a set up and that he was going to be gated. Meaning they charge you as you leave the jail with new charges. His relax time was later than mine.

Just because I was able to take a deeper breath, to relax my shoulders a little, and was so very-over-the-top happy to have my son within my reach, didn't mean he felt exactly the same way. But all I wanted to do was get him in the car and get the hell out of there as fast as I could. I had wanted this moment every single time I left a prison visit, and this time it was finally happening.

I wanted to throw all his stuff in the car, grab him, and drive away as fast as possible, just in case it was a dream, or something changed, and I did just that. I actually told my husband, "Let's get out of here as quick as possible."

He obliged, but our "get away" came to a screeching halt when Drake told us to stop the car, he felt sick. We thought he was kidding, but he wasn't. He was experiencing motion sickness. After all, he hadn't been in a moving vehicle in a good year and half. I am sure he wanted to leave as quickly as I did, to leave that place in our dust; however, there was nothing fast about getting out of there. I hadn't thought about him not being in a moving vehicle, or the stress of being around many people on the ferry ride, instead of in a controlled environment around just a few people, day in and day out. There were so many things that I did not consider or that even entered my mind, these being the big ones.

On the ferry, there were about 1,000 people all moving about. Because his world was so contained until that moment, once we were on the ferry, going to the ferry cafeteria, he held onto the back of my shirt like a small child. It was cute and sad at the same time. We entered the cafeteria line, and my husband asked Drake what he wanted. After he told us, my husband told him to go grab us a table. Drake looked at him with complete shock and said, "I'm not going out there by myself. I'm good right here, thanks." Another moment where we chuckled, but he was serious. So I went with him to find a table, he was that uncomfortable on his own in the sea of people.

The big crowd was way too overstimulating for him. I was concerned on how he would react if someone bumped into him or him into someone. I didn't know if he was so over-stimulated that one thing might set him off, if his emotions were so raw that he would react. I am sure he didn't either, which is why he stayed close. I also didn't know if someone would recognize him or us. I didn't know how his behaviour would be in this kind of situation. If someone would say something and if it would upset him, or me, so I was a little on edge myself.

Maybe that was the moment I realized my suffering and his suffering were two different things. For me, bringing him home was the most satisfying, gratitude-filled experience. I know he was happy to see me and to be free, but his response to that freedom was different than mine. How could it not be?

Despite all these concerns, I realized I was happy. Finally, here were some emotions other than anger finding their way to me. I knew this had to be a good thing, and I was only just beginning to realize how dark my thoughts had gotten. I thought, man, it has been a long time since I felt like this.

But neither his nor my own journey was over yet. Once I brought him home, I was still protective of myself and of him. I didn't allow anyone into our world at first, especially considering the way that people had behaved while he was incarcerated. I thought that if people didn't have good things to say while he was inside, they sure in the heck were not coming around to visit once he was outside again. I wanted him to know that we loved him even though he had made some poor choices. I wanted to bring people back into his social bubble slowly. We had things to consider and adapt to.

One of the first group events I held was a big family potluck. Most family members showed, but we had a few that didn't make it. That was okay by me, everyone was entitled to their thoughts as long as they kept them and their opinions to themselves. I didn't want to hear bad things then and I don't want to hear them now. I didn't want the negativity around myself or Drake, and if they couldn't find the positivity in their hearts to show up, then they could just stay away.

The potluck ended up being a good integration into the outside world. It was safe, it was loving, and it was kind. It made my heart happy, it made me feel grateful and it made me feel blessed by the people who did show up. I was and am so very thankful for those in my family that came that day and just loved us. Whether they did it for him, for Kaylee, for me, or to make themselves feel good, it didn't matter. They showed up at a time when I so needed them. It wasn't just my parents, it was aunts, uncles, and cousins.

I needed the support possibly more than Drake did. I needed it to know that people had our backs. After feeling as if I was unsupported, so isolated, and alone, this gathering allowed me to move out of my narrow-minded self-absorbed grief.

To start to break down some walls that I had built so solid and high out of self-preservation. Seeing everyone there also allowed me the space to see that I wasn't the only one who was there for Drake himself. I knew then that if for any reason I wasn't able to be there for my son, that family would be.

It's not always true that family is there for some family members. Even family can feel distaste for certain things, have strong opinions and let go of a person. I've seen it and been a part of it with some family members in regards to Drake, so those that showed up that day were especially important. I knew they loved us despite all of my hurt, anger, and despair. I knew in my heart of hearts that if push came to shove, they would be on our side to support us, not necessarily the situation that transpired to lead us here. It's important not to confuse the two.

That day they told me, with their actions, that when nothing else in your world feels solid or concrete, we will be the rock you need. When your lungs are struggling for breath, then we will be the air to help you breathe. And when the ground is crumpling under your feet, we will be the solid place on which you safely land. I know this isn't how it goes for everyone, and for that I feel terribly sad. I wish everyone had the love of a strong family to support them.

After years of being in the darkest place possible, I had more or less ended up as something of a recluse, spending less and less time with people and most likely not being that pleasant when I did spend time. No doubt, I was a total douchebag. Yet here they were showing up when I asked, loving me and helping me adapt once again to another phase in my life. I am not sure why I have been blessed with a family so large, so encouraging, so kind, and so able to love the unlovable, but all I could do during that potluck was say, "Thank you."

Thank you is not enough, but it has the simplicity and the graciousness of what you want to express. All the same, it lacks the depth of the gratitude your soul feels, and I hope they know how good they made me feel that day and every day since. Loving the unlovable is really a challenge, it is quite a gift to be able to do so.

From that point on, our integration into society seemed to go well. Drake adjusted pretty well, starting with that big gathering. Of course, that was all family, so I'm sure that made some difference. I still was a little edgy, watching, listening, ready to pounce if anyone should happen to say anything that would upset him. I remember watching with sadness in my heart, looking at my boy and watching him watch all the family members moving about and how hesitant he was at first, how cautious he was with himself and his behaviour, and his words.

I thought how horrible it must be for him to be so young and have so much to carry; to have made so many choices, one in particular that is going to affect you for the rest of your life. As I watched my son, I could not help but feel a deep conflict between joy and deep sorrow. To this day I feel that way. I think I will probably feel that way for the rest of my life, just as the choices he made will affect him for the rest of his life, as a burden on his own heart that he will carry forever. With the way society judges people, it is a stigma he will have to endure going forward in his life.

So, from that moment on, with my family around me and Drake out of prison, I'd love to say that I was adjusting well and getting back into the swing of things; however, that would be a big fat lie.

You'd think you'd move forward then. You have a misconception inside that just because your loved one is out of prison you will go back to being normal. But despite the fact that you are relieved that he or she is home, you cannot really get on with things. I found myself still being protective, deeply protective, not just toward Drake but to my daughter as well.

People were so cruel with the words they used against Drake when speaking to Kaylee while he was in prison, I worried how they would treat and talk to her now that he was out.

I worried about heading into the world myself, which I still had no real desire to do. I was still trying to get my footing on some pretty unstable ground. I still found it difficult to talk to people, even though I expected myself to do better, and along with others having that expectation of me. Or at least I felt that they did.

I worried that someone would hurt him for hurting someone else. If they did, would he be able to handle it, or would it push him over the edge? Would he be able to function in society? Would he be employable? Would anyone give him a chance? Was he going to be able to stay on track after the things he had been through?

All of that kept running through my head. I just worried about how my son was going to get by, how was he going to deal with the consequences of his choices out in the world when not confined to a cell. He had missed out on a time when people learn so much. While incarcerated he didn't get to learn some basic life skills that I am not sure if he can ever recoup. I know that a lot of those who have been incarcerated end up feeling that same way, like not knowing how to write a check, practical things like that.

I worried and hoped that my son wanted to stay out of prison as much as I wanted him to, because it was my understanding that some former prisoners find it simply easier to go back to prison and live the life they learned there, rather than learning how to function in the "real" world. While he was on probation, I knew he would make the three-year commitment of staying out of trouble. During that probation time, hopefully be able to get his life on track. But nothing was guaranteed.

I thought for sure once he was out, I was going to be over the moon, happy, all the restraints that were keeping me in this one spot would be lifted. But while things had shifted, and the sky wasn't so black, I wasn't as elated as I thought I was going to be.

To some extent, this is because you have been so disconnected with your own feelings; you have to be, to just function. Having my emotions and feeling locked down became a normal way of living for me. I really could only deal with a little bit of my emotions at one time.

I still do that. If I sat down and I told someone the story about Drake, and really told the details, the visual of the stabbing would be impossible to digest. I can only digest a little bit at a time, or I would be a mess.

So, at that point I had to disconnect to keep going. Even to this day, it is gut wrenching for me to say that my son split a man open and his intestines fell out. I remember being in a first aid class for work a few years ago, discussing minor wound care. For some reason, the instructor talked about how to care for someone if they were stabbed and their intestines were to fall outside of them. It is a different type of care if the intestines completely come out than if they are *about* to fall out. It was unexpected to hear something like that, as I wouldn't consider either to be a "minor" wound.

The instructor said that as first aid attendants, we would put the wounded person on a spine board/stretcher bed and place the intestines on top of the person. You would not try to put them back inside the injured person.

I could feel the sweat on my neck, the heat rising up my face. I didn't know which was winning, the feeling of nausea or the urge to cry. I was looking around to see if anyone was staring at me. I had to talk myself through it, reminding myself that the people in the class did not know me. They did not know that the instructor was describing the same terrible injury my son had inflicted on that man on his 21st birthday that placed him in prison.

I wanted to vomit and pass out, but I had to convince myself I was okay, and needed to make it through the rest of the class. I have never wanted to leave a place so badly. As soon as it was finished, I left the classroom as quickly as I could, got to my car and cried. I cried so many tears, tears that I had not allowed to come for many years.

It was the first time I truly allowed the impact of my son's behaviour to wash over me. I understood that I had been stuffing my feelings while Drake was in prison. I knew that I was denying any of my own emotions or thoughts about the situation. Feeling like if I allowed the impact of his choices to affect me, I would feel like I had betrayed him in some way, not being of service, unable to help or defend. I came home and sent an email to my psychologist, because I knew in that moment that it was the first and only time I had PTSD regarding Drake's situation. I knew in that moment that I needed help.

At that point, it had been six years since Drake's arrest and yet it was the first time that I allowed myself to feel, really feel, to have the emotional connection to what had happened that night. It was the first time that I let it all come crashing down upon me.

I'd spent so much time just defending Drake, but I knew in that moment that I didn't need to anymore. What I needed to do was look at the reality of what had happened, the severity of what he had done. I allowed it all to wash over me in the safety of my car with no outside influence.

I sometimes find it amazing that I had gone so long just putting one foot in front of the other, tackling each day as it came, always on guard, always ready to defend, always ready to pounce, always keeping my own feelings at bay. No wonder I was exhausted.

I have shared with you the pain of not sharing daily life with my son because he was imprisoned. I've described the pain of others' behaviours toward myself or my family, the heartache of the insensitive words that people said, the grief and loss of my son's absence, along with loss of friends and relationships along the way.

Before that first aid class, things had improved, don't get me wrong. But they had not reached the level I had hoped for emotionally. I was finally able to function with a bit more ease. For the three years Drake was on probation, it seemed like it was just another phase with different sorts of concerns and challenges, and more emotions that I was struggling with.

My son didn't stay at home with me that long even during that period. He adapted to outside life and his freedom far more quickly than I did. He started to venture out, socializing, finding work and moving along with his life. When he would go out, I would worry about his interactions; when he looked for work, my heart would sink because I knew how hard it would be for him and all the work restrictions he would have due to being in prison.

As our circumstances changed, my heart and head seemed to find more conflict between them. But my logical side won, and I put one foot in front of the other. I helped my son with things he would need to function in day-to-day life. I helped him write a résumé, helped him with getting a car, took him to look for work.

Some of those are moments I look back on and smile about now, such as when he applied for his first job at age 24. I gave him a hug before he went in. I smile now not because it was cute, I smile because I love that he showed his vulnerability to me. Even though he had been through shit, he still relied on me for support, and he still trusted me.

It makes me smile that even though he was in a place where so many get hard and disconnected, he still had heart. He took whatever job he could get, he got a girlfriend, and with those steps, then he wanted more.

He looked for a better job and thankfully someone gave him a chance. Obtaining that new job is another moment that makes me smile because Drake was honest. His boss initially didn't want to hire him, but Drake told him the truth about where he had been and why and asked the man to at least meet him, and if he didn't like him after that, then fair enough.

That was pretty ballsy of him. Because of that action, Drake was employed with that fellow for a few years, doing contractor work, which a decent job. During that time, Drake started a family and continued to move forward. For a short time, I allowed myself to enjoy the little bit of normalcy we experienced while Drake was on probation. He was starting a family and all those good things.

That said, after the three relatively peaceful years of Drake's probation, we have had other troubles.

Drake had a few more struggles over the last few years with drugs and alcohol. It was just very recently that Drake went into treatment so he could be fully present and be the best father he could possibly be for his children, my grandchildren. Drake's son had a serious health problem and was only recently given a stable diagnosis despite having very large brain cysts. He'd undergone brain surgery at just one year of age, but for now it was just wait and see on any further surgery, so we can catch our breath. Knowing that his son was stable helped Drake to find the incentive and purpose to get clean and sober.

Christopher, unfortunately, has been active in his addiction for the last four years. I did see him just recently in a group of homeless people on the street. I called out his name, but he didn't want to look at me, even though I asked him to. He didn't want to hug me because he said he was dirty, but I hugged him anyway.

I knew he was uneasy; he told me he tries to avoid me, so I don't have to see him like this. I reassured him that I loved him no matter what condition he is in and that I always will. I told him that I love him much, and we parted ways.

As much as I would have loved to throw him in my car, take him home, and keep him safe, I knew I could not.

I know that the journey I am on with the boys has not been an easy one. I have heard people's thoughts and opinions of homeless, criminals, and addicts, knowing or not that my family is deeply affected by it. I watch people on a daily basis make decisions on how they can avoid eye contact or sneak by someone they find less desirable, dirty, or unhealthy. With this I have always taken the opportunity to educate or share from my point of view. I have always thought if I could help just one person see things from a different perspective, through someone else's eyes, and it could somehow make the world better for my boys, then I would take it.

Example: One time while in a leadership course in Vancouver for the Liquor Distribution Branch (LDB), at the end of the course we had to do an education piece, a training lesson. I had planned to do a demonstration on proper procedure of box cutting, safety of blade handling, and such. Though, when I was driving to the course in the morning with another classmate, she mentioned that she been downtown the night before. She, like many I have heard, talked about all the homeless, the drug addicts, the filth with disgust. I said nothing in response, though I could feel the vibration of my emotions course through my body, I just smiled at her with sad eyes and in that moment I changed my choice of educational piece to talk to the class about.

The instructor comes by to check on your lesson and see if you need any assistance. She strongly discouraged my topic.

She told me that changing someone's perception or mind, no matter the topic, was extremely difficult. She felt that my topic of addiction and homeless would be disappointing for myself and didn't know how I would be able to educate change on the topic. It didn't matter; I had to take the opportunity.

One of the clearest understandings I learned from my experience with the boys is that everything is an opportunity for growth. That no matter where, when, or with who, the conversation that includes them and any part of our journey will be uncomfortable for everyone in the room. I have lived the stigma that encompasses what kind of person people believe me to be because of who and how my children are. I sit in the judgment of many with the publicity of the case as well as a small town. Those that know me and those that do not. I understood fully well what it was like to be looked at with remorse, with shame that I was unable to be or do better. The disbelief in some that this was my life, I didn't seem like the type. I usually allowed these awkward and uncomfortable moments to produce themselves organically (like the morning drive); this would be my first time putting myself in a room full of people and starting the conversation myself. For the first time, I was making a choice to talk about the awkwardness, the shame, the hurt, the misunderstanding and being that I was the one doing the talking the silence of the others in the room wasn't as cutting as when you're in the midst of a conversation when the topic arises. It was mentioned to me that this felt self-serving when I wrote this part; I want to inform you, there is nothing, and I mean nothing, self-serving about putting yourself in a very uncomfortable position, exposing your deep hurts, sadness with a room full of strangers in a hope that they may view someone that comes into their sight, store, street corner in a slightly different light. I knew it was a long shot, the instructor even said so; however, for the love of my child I was more than willing to sit in that chair, shaky voice trying to speak strongly and clear, nervous and trying not to fidget too much with the amount of energy flowing through, and dear God the amount of sweat beading off you. It's a place I don't choose to put myself often or ever before, and a topic un-talked about, because it comes with the attachment and stigma of bad parenting, bad people, and shame. It was important to me to rise above whatever emotional conditions that myself and society had attached to the views of homeless and drug addicts. If I could help someone see an addict or a homeless person in just a slightly different light, then it was going to be worth it. Mainly, if they could see my Christopher in a different light, it would be worth it. And maybe that part is self-serving because really it was about my boy.

I started off by asking them if they had children. Then I asked them if they were ever disappointed in their child. I asked them if they ever became protective when someone hurt that child physically, mentally, or emotionally. And as most people do, they said yes.

I said, "Today, June 14, is my Christopher's birthday and much like you I wanted to protect my child from any additional pain from others. At the beginning of the day, I was going to talk to you about something far less personal and heartbreaking; however, with a conversation I had while driving to class, it changed my mind."

I went on to tell them that I had not seen Christopher in nine months at that point, and not because I didn't want to see him, but because I was unable to find him. I had looked desperately. I told them that Christopher had fallen into addiction, his drugs of choice were heroin and speed, that about a year ago he started to use with his biological mother. YES, you read that correctly—his biological mother. I talked about his living on the streets, wearing the same clothes, same shoes, no showers, no bed. I talked about how tough it must be for him as well as how tough it is for me and how heartbroken I was. I talked about how much I loved him, and I talked about how sad I was that he had made the choices he had made.

I made it clear that despite everything, he was still my son, I still wanted him to be okay, and that each and every night I worried about him. I worried that he would freeze in the winter or overheat in summer. I worried that he would overdose, and no one would know where he was. I worried about what kind of trouble he would get into to get money to survive and stay in his addiction.

I then equated it to our jobs. I was no longer working for the ferry, I now work for BC Liquor, a regulatory agency. People come in scraping up what little money they have to pay for their alcohol addiction, so it was easy for me to discuss this issue with the people I work with. We see addicts coming in to buy their booze, even if they are almost homeless digging in their pockets to get just enough to buy a can of beer. Or maybe they are the homeless bringing in bags and bags of empty cans to return for money to get their addiction filled.

I talked about our behaviours in society and in the workplace, the way we talk about "those people," talking down to them, or walking behind them spraying Lysol while in the store, all the while, feeling justified in actions like that.

I asked them if they would do that if it were a well-dressed man or woman who had on too much perfume or cologne? How was it ok to spray Lysol behind a pungent smell of your distaste when we believed they were less than, compared to it not being ok to spray behind a well-off individual whose smell was just as unpleasant to you.

With tears rolling down my face, I asked them to think about me next time they wanted to do that to a customer they felt they could treat poorly because they stunk, were homeless, or an addict. I wanted them to think of me and how much I love Christopher and how it would break my heart to know that people were treating him like that when he was already so low. If they couldn't think of him humanely then think about me. He was somebody's somebody, someone's son, someone's brother, someone's friend, someone's someone. And someone loves him.

I reminded them that sometimes a little kindness can make a big difference in someone's day. Would they judge Chris less if they knew his biological mother got him hooked on drugs? Would they judge him less if they knew that he taught his brother to read and write, that he was protective and caring about his sister, that he struggled daily with himself about how he turned out and with the demons he fights? I hear it time and time again about the addicted, that they make choices, and yes, they do and so do we. We should choose to be kind, choose to be empathetic, choose to be better. You don't know anyone's story and don't be so sure that it can't happen to you. In a single moment anyone's life can change.

Much like myself, most of the class was in tears. It resonated with many; even though I am sure they will likely fall back into old patterns, I also know they will remember my story. They will remember me speaking from my heart and hearing the sadness and pain, but what will move them to choose to act differently is the love. The love that I poured out about a homeless man, who unlike most of the homeless they know, this one had a name, and they could physically see I was pained by his absence. It made it real for them. Some I could tell felt embarrassed for me, shame, for me it was worth exposing my wounds and being vulnerable to judgment to create that opportunity for change. A different perspective on how one might view a homeless person, an addict like my Christopher.

EIGHT

SOCIETY AND YOUR EMOTIONS

One of the most valuable things I learned and had to emotionally deal with through the whole process, more so after sentencing, was while Drake's situation was affecting me deeply, it was not my responsibility. In no way was I responsible for my children's choices, not at this age. Your child's choices are not yours. You have to process it all, you pull it apart, chew it up, spit it out, and try to reassemble to see if you can make any sense of it all. You over analyze everything and examine every nook and cranny with a high intensity magnifying glass.

Did they come from a bad home? Was I a bad mom? Could I have done better? Did I encourage this type of behaviour? You can see parts of you in your children's behaviour traits, attitudes, and beliefs; is this part of you as well? You are the parent after all, so do you have to own some of it? No, however, you will be in turmoil about it for a while until you realize you are not. Unless of course you are and then you have to look at yourself. My children did not come from a bad home, and I know that I was not a bad mom. I love my children with every ounce of love I have inside of me. My children were an absolute priority in my world to a point that I may have lost a bit of me making them the most important. Most of my major life choices revolved around my children, including leaving a great government job so I could be more available to them while they were going through tougher stages while growing up.

I provided them with unconditional love; I provided them with the most stable and safe environment I could. Most of all, what I knew to be true was that no one could love my children more than I did, and no one could care for them better than me. I wasn't perfect, I am human after all, but I was as good as I could be and did the best that I could and contrary to how this situation makes you feel, it was enough.

In spite of knowing this, my logical and emotional parts did not mesh. Logically I could understand a lot, emotionally not so much. Your logic and emotions don't really get along in the beginning...ha, who am I kidding? They don't get along so well through the journey of a child's incarceration at all. Though I knew logically this was not my responsibility, it surely did not stop the pain and heartache. You ache when you go to bed, you ache when you wake up, and you ache in the time that you are unable to sleep because the ache is so intense that sleep eludes you.

The pain is so intense that you're not really sure how you're still breathing and yet you are. I have had pain in my life, and what I thought was a heartache, but it was in the moments of my son's arrest and sentencing and the years that he was incarcerated, that I realized what heartache really was, and that a broken heart is a very real thing.

Losing a relationship with your child in this way isn't something that I am able to describe. It isn't like a loss of a friendship; I mean it is because they are your buds but they are more than just a friendship. It isn't like losing a spouse, least in the only way I know of losing a spouse which was divorce and that sucked, was emotional and hurt my heart, but this... this was deeper, it felt more personal. Maybe more ownership to it because it's your child. It is something deep within your soul, something stronger and deeper than any other relationship experience you have, possibly because your child is in part your creation. When they hurt, you hurt for them; when you feel helpless from pain about them, it breaks your heart.

The loss of time, the loss of unspoken words, the loss of hugs, the loss of togetherness, special moments like birthdays, holidays, and most of all the loss of memories that will never be created. This breaks your heart and something deep within you knows that life is never going to be the same. It won't be the same, not for you, not for them, not for anyone involved, not today, not tomorrow and not any day in the near future. You become sort of numb, you move through the days in a fog. Honestly, nothing seems right, the sky isn't as blue, the sun isn't as bright, everything seems to have a bit of a dull haze to it all.

The first few months were horrible, and I would like to say the worst; however, it didn't work like that. They were all horrible: the days, the months, the years; they just did not lighten up. Each day brought its own challenge, moments that you know your child would have enjoyed, simple moments that you once took for granted but will not ever again. Every special occasion, there was not a day where you did not feel loss, the pain and discomfort of your broken heart. With each day you wondered, how the hell did we end up here? And when the heck am I going to feel better? Will I ever?

I wasn't sure how to deal with feelings that would randomly come crashing in, out of the blue. The range of emotions I felt zinging through my body in a single day were completely crazy. There was no consistency in how they came about, what triggered them, or how they would affect me. The emotions themselves were pretty consistent. The main emotions being sadness; however, there were some other constants that presented themselves on a daily basis. Sadness's best buds used to make a pretty regular appearance; you may know them as anger and frustration. Disappointment would tag along and to make sure you held onto shame so loneliness could join in. I realize now this is all part of grief; however, back then I had no idea. All I knew was sadness was always there, poking me in the heart, over and over through the course of the day, each and everyday. Sadness was most definitely my constant companion.

It was a strange feeling this sadness that walked within me each day. It wasn't your feelings got hurt kind of sad, you know the one I mean, like when someone says something and it's like the sting of a jab on the chin. Where it sets you back and stings a little. You give it a rub, think dang that hurt and it does for a few days but it heals, and you move on. This sad is so heavy that movement is hard, everything is hard, it takes up so much of your body that very little else could make its way in. The weight of it leaves you feeling exhausted and that happens just from trying to get out of bed, not even dealing with carrying it around with you all day. If a laugh managed to find its way out, it wasn't a full joy laugh, it was logical, that was funny, I need to laugh, more robotic than anything. It wasn't like the sadness of depression where you want to hurt yourself or no longer exist. Though at times you will most definitely feel low and have that lonely feeling like depression; however, no medication is going to be able to help you because it isn't depression, it's grief! All other emotions were taken over by the grief's heavy weight of sadness.

Things are never what you expect in a time like this, though to be honest I don't really know what I expected them to be like...maybe more supportive, more compassion, less judgment, less ache; whatever it was I was expecting it was not what I was experiencing. Despite how hard all this was for me, I found that I kept a lot to myself. Not because I didn't want to share, but because people were not open to it. It was like I was walking around without a beating heart, no colour, no life within me, and yet no one noticed the grey that had taken over my skin or the joy that had left my body. I felt very invisible.

Occasionally, something would trigger the emotions. It could be anything; however, this one particular time when at work, it was Michael Bublé's song, "Home." No matter how hard I tried I could not stop the tears from forming, from falling. It didn't seem to matter that I was in an uncomfortable non-understanding environment, they were going to spill out anyway. I had to leave and hurry to the safety of my home, in order to let my tears really fall where there was no judgment. Even if I was alone in the house, that was more comforting than being alone in a place full of people. Even today this song still pulls at my heartstrings and brings up emotions of this time for me.

The months go by, and somehow you think you ought to be feeling better, but yet you do not. Time doesn't heal your wound. The world around you is changing and growing, and you are stuck. I am not sure why you think you ought to feel better, maybe because people expect you to feel better, so you think you should too. Possibly because of the way people talk to you or treat you; possibly because society indicates that you ought to be feeling better, so you think you should be as well. Though the expectation was to feel better or not have this impact me as deeply as it did, I tried to move on, but none of my feelings let up. So while the first months were the worst in many ways, the impact and the pain continued, with none of it getting "easier."

A few months in I did start to go out, not because I wanted to because I forced myself to. The first time I ventured out, I kept it simple to somewhere that I normally would love to go. I went to my local favourite coffee shop. I thought this will be great, I know it, I like it, it's a place I feel comfortable and enjoy. I can sit and write or read while I enjoy a coffee. I was soooooo wrong. It was nothing like the experience I had before everything happened. It felt completely different. I went in alone, and this time, I felt alone.

I felt awkward, uncomfortable, and even though I brought nothing with me except a debit card, I felt completely weighed down by the weight of it in my pocket. I was exhausted by the time I sat down at the table. I did not last there long, and it did not give me the pleasure or normalcy I'd hoped. So, I went back home, where it wasn't so obvious to me how alone and isolated I was.

I didn't try to go out too much because I couldn't handle it emotionally. With my emotions so raw and the blanket of sadness tamping down the anger, I couldn't trust that something would trigger the emotions and the anger coming out with vengeance. I was angry with so many things, the lack of compassion, lack of kindness, lack of empathy, what seemed to anger me the most was that I seemed invisible. Sometimes I wanted to jump up and down, scream at the top of my lungs to see if anyone would notice me, acknowledge me and my emotions. I could not understand why my heartbreak was so invisible to so many and that brought out the anger, which was really just a mask for the deep sadness and loneliness. There were no good distractions.

In October, three months after my son was arrested, people at work were putting together a gift basket for someone whose father had passed away. I was asked if I wanted to donate. I said sure, and then I couldn't help it, I said, "How come I didn't get a basket?"

The woman who asked me to donate looked right at me and told me that I hadn't lost anyone in my family. There was that zing of pain right to my stomach that knocks the wind out of you, and I looked at her and said, "It sure feels like it."

I am pretty sure that grief is grief just like pain is pain, so I wasn't sure what the differences were between his grief and mine. I understood the obvious; his father was never coming back, mind you neither were my boys, not the same ones that went in anyway. I understood that his had an ending, mine did not. Mine was an uncertainty on if and when they got out and I would be able to see them again if they survived their prison sentences, and the fellow they were collecting for unfortunately was never going to see his father again, only within his memory. Those differences I could see, but there was another difference and the one I still struggle to understand. He, the other person, grieving his father's death, was allowed and even encouraged to show and feel his grief, but mine was considered to be "not okay" and totally dismissed.

It was hard to not build resentment toward my coworkers, I would like to tell you that I was super successful and was able to rise above it all and that I built special bonds with them; however, I would be totally lying. I did become resentful, maybe even petty and I would like to tell you that I found forgiveness in their ignorance; however, I did not, not for a long while after. Here I was completely broken, receiving no compassion, but if there was something happening that they found acceptable, such as a tragedy of death or an accident among their peers, they were ready to rally and show compassion and care.

How is one supposed to deal with that? Did I not have enough already on my plate that I was somehow supposed to rise above shitty behaviour? I didn't trust them to be kind or show empathy, they had already proven they could not, least not toward my situation. I definitely was not going to leave myself in any vulnerable or exposed situations around them, another reason I probably didn't show up for work much during this time. It was hard enough getting out of bed let alone having to deal with the judgment of eight hours from the people you worked with. Ones that ran to management the moment you had a tone, mood, or a slight bit of discontent. I think back and wonder if I could have done it differently and of course I think sure I could have. If I am being brutally honest, I could not have.

I wish I would have been able to rise above the pain, shame, and judgments of my coworkers. I wish I could have educated them on how terribly sad and difficult everything was for me, just as I did in my group class about my homeless son. What I realize now is that the problem wasn't me having to rise above, I was doing the complete best I could. They sure did not expect the fellow who lost his dad to rise above and move past his pain quickly. The problem was that I had faith and trust in these people that I worked with, that I had a false understanding of what it meant to be on a team, the problem was I expected them to behave like I would. Even in my grief I was able to show empathy for others, I still know when the coworker's dad passed and for many years after I would check in and see if he was doing okay on that day. I understand that now, that our expectations are that of what we are capable of giving, and when the people we value or share our time with fall short we become disappointed. When you're already broken that disappointment can be detrimental to your well-being.

Maybe part of the problem was they didn't know everything about the situation, it was so tight-lipped, besides the media bits in the paper and on the news. Which you know they don't always give most accurate information. Maybe they couldn't get past the judgment because they had never had the experience I was going through. Possibly, much like myself, it was just toooo much to process and therefore it was easier for them to look at me, project their thoughts and opinions, than it was to see my wounds. I cannot tell you if my teammates would have shown up more if it would have made a difference. I cannot tell you because I do not know what that looks like. From where I was standing it looked supportive and compassionate for the other fellow. Would a basket have made my pain go away? No! Though it may have made me feel like I was thought of, cared for, and most importantly, seen.

I was so busy defending loving my sons, advocating for mental health and addiction, or defending myself or family that

I never got the opportunity to process my own heart and feelings. I never was able to understand or process my own emotions around my sons' actions, let alone have an opportunity to explain to anyone else. I did not examine or touch on my own emotions about the situation until much later.

I wish there would have been the opportunity to address that big, hard pill to swallow, the one that my son had stabbed someone. When I say stabbed, it really isn't that accurate, it was more like a slice, a very large gaping wound, one that was so large and so deep that the fellow's intestines fell outside of his body. Causing such severe damage that he almost killed the man. I am not sure I am painting a very good picture of the horrific-ness of this situation. As I type this I want to vomit. It still makes me sick to my stomach and gives me the sweats.

Having the dynamic that your child did this, wondering what the hell happened, and not having the opportunity to process farther than that because you get caught up in all the other crap that comes along with it. Defending the harsh judgments and basically just trying not to drown in the sea of pain prevents you from being able to process sooner. I was so busy trying to survive while protecting my own heart, I suppressed my son's actions for a long time.

I believe because shame is attached to your situation, the emotions that you are trying so hard to deal with get pushed down. You do not get the opportunity to feel because you are so busy doing all the other things as mentioned earlier: protecting, defending, justifying, surviving. All the while you are so incredibly sad and barely an opportunity to feel it. Let alone the other emotions, horror, anguish, disbelief, shock, and anger. Those don't even get to the surface until much later on.

It was hard to process my own thoughts on the situation when I had so many people telling me theirs, and I was in a situation where people were expecting me to be better than what I was. I mean seriously, not even a week or so later and coworkers were complaining about my attitude. I realize as I write this that I still have some resentment toward my coworkers with the lack of care and how they treated me during this terrible time in my life. I worked at four different government liquor stores, with over 70 employees; you would think that someone, anyone, would be able to see the pain, step up, and offer some assistance, support or something. Approximately eight months into my situation an old timer decided to break the ice. While in the back warehouse he talked about the taboo subject, my son. It was more to poke fun at me than a conversation. I actually think he mocked me about having a (utility) knife in my hand. Something about if the apple didn't fall far from the tree, but in a lighthearted way. Probably not the most appropriate way to shift the mood, but I understood that he was trying to ease my pain and the heaviness I carried within me.

Maybe he couldn't understand everything I was going through; however, he opened a door for me to be a little bit freer within my work environment. To feel like I had at least one ally. That I wasn't so isolated and alone. He was okay with me being angry, sad, and angry all over again if something triggered me. He would say the most ridiculous things, more for the reactions of others, but it would make me smile. Even if it was only for a moment, he honestly found a way to bring a bit of normalcy back into my world. But he was just one person among many and my time at work was not easy, life wasn't easy, and for a while I thought the distraction of working would somehow be good, it was not, it was worse.

I took time off from work and the human resources disability case manager would call me every week wanting to know when I was going to go back to work. What was my plan to get back? She told me that my attendance was an issue. Ya, no shit! I remember it adding to my frustration of already being misunderstood and unvalidated in my pain. I remember saying to my husband, "Do you think they would do this if it was a death in the family? Or if I was really sick? Fighting for my well-being with something other than my mental state?" My mental health was not okay. I was like a fully loaded gun, half-cocked, and ready for the trigger to be pulled so the sadness and anger could fully blast out of the chamber. I see it now, how narrow-minded one can get in grief, then I didn't realize what was happening to me. I just knew I felt alone, invisible, misunderstood, and ANGRY. No one in my work environment needed that misdirected anger and I needed to not feel so ostracized in an already lonely situation.

So, when I stopped working it was because I realized that the best place for me was home. I had no benefits; therefore, I wasn't paid and I was losing seniority. But I was a mess and doing the best I could to get into a better, healthier place, and though I know I was an employee and the human resources department had to do their job, it only came across like I was a number on their books. Any care for me as a person was lost in the process of making a buck.

I remember that my human resources department once called two days in a row, and each time we talked about why I was off work. I explained that my doctor signed me off because I was unable to function well, that he felt that I was suffering from severe anxiety and depression due to my life situation. That he felt that I was unable to deal with the added stresses of being out in the work force in my current condition. That I was connecting with him weekly and we were working out a plan. He wanted me to take medication and I wanted to try counselling, which I had started. I let her know that my doctor suggested that it wasn't in anyone's best interest for me to be at work right now and that I was doing my best to get myself healthy so I could return.

It was ridiculous, but the HR rep didn't know that she'd already spoken to me from one day to the next. She even said, "Oh my God, you're the second person I've talked to that has two boys in prison…"

I replied that I thought it was me she was talking about, but she kept saying, "Nope. I just spoke to that person yesterday."

I then said that was me, "I talked to you yesterday."

"No, I'm sure it wasn't," she replied. Sigh…Of course, that was me!

I realized it was pointless to say anything to correct her after a while, so I just repeated the same conversation we had the day before and hung up. If I ever thought I was valued or considered anything more than a number, that day confirmed I was not. For a person in my mental state experiencing the heartache that I was, that conversation with HR just pushed me farther down the rabbit hole, it left me feeling more deflated and unimportant than I already did.

As it was, I was barely able to tread water; I was so exhausted and weak that I felt like I was drowning. Thankfully, after firing a crappy counsellor, I found a really great one and what a blessing he was for me. In our first session he listened to my story I shared about being off work and how my doctor thought that I needed medication because he thought I was depressed. I told him about my struggles, my anger, my frustration, and my deep, deep sorrow. You know in these moments of counselling is when a counsellor will normally reflect everything back to you, so you can process and learn how you're feeling. But when I was done talking, he said very little except for, "Do you know anything about the cycle of grief? Because what it sounds like to me, dear, is that you are grieving." He talked about grief and what it was. My first session and he was able to validate some of my feelings. Which helped me to feel more without judgment about myself and the whole situation.

My counsellor showed me that it was totally normal to feel as awful as I was during these turbulent stages of grief. I wasn't depressed, I wasn't unreasonable. It was okay for me to want to be validated in how I was feeling. It was okay for me feel sorry for myself, to feel sad, to just be. My counsellor was actually an art therapist. I am not sure if that made more of a difference in his training, though it was a gift for me because I had just gotten into painting with my girlfriend, Kari. So at times when I had no words, we did art.

My friend Kari, my first support and survival system, was also there for me. Both she and my counsellor allowed me to be, simply be. They encouraged me to explore my feelings, to have empathy and knowledge in this journey. Instead of spending time defending myself, I was able to express, examine my own feelings and emotions. They both helped me move through pain that I could not make sense of. Without them I would not have fared well at all.

My friend was such a gift. I know it would have been so much worse for me if she wasn't in my life at this time. She had experienced a loss of a child, in a different way than my own loss, when her child passed away. To this day it still amazes me how she shared her pain to educate me in mine. She was and still is one of the loving lights in my life. She encouraged me to spend time in my emotions. We would paint, chat, and paint some more together. Between her and my art therapist, painting became an outlet of expression.

When we would paint together, she encouraged me to feel instead of think, to let it flow, which got me out of my head. To just let the brush move. Our first time painting together, I was extremely rigid; I loved how free she was in her own expression.

She would tell me, "Just paint and see how it turns out." So, I painted, kept painting, and painted a lot. I love that she gave me that gift. I now have so many canvases, some huge ones that I have painted and display. When life becomes heavy and I need an outlet, I paint; I can get very lost in it. It allows me to be free and just be in a moment. In those very troubling times, painting is better than any drug my doctor would have prescribed.

She would share with me her own losses and pain and tell

me about moving on and letting go. She was so smart about what I was experiencing. Despite her own loss, she told me she felt bad for me, because she knew long before I did that my grief was going to be different than that of most people. She knew I would be stuck in the grieving process likely until after Drake was released. There would just be no closure until then.

I didn't get it, but she did. I kept thinking that I was grateful he was alive, and I assumed things would be easier than they were. She was a hundred percent right, however. Because both my sons and I were locked in prisons, separate and yet together, neither of us able to move beyond the point we were at. They, behind walls that dictated what they did, and for me, my heart unable to move any farther in healing than it was.

My friend taught me so much, she shared how she managed and grew through her grief, and encouraged me to grow as well, and she did so with so much grace. I love her so very much for so many reasons, mostly because when I was at my most unlovable moments, she loved me. I know how rare it is to have this kind of support.

Yet at the time, even though I loved her and appreciated her unconditional love and support, I still reverted to spending more time alone. I am pretty sure it has something to do with getting caught in the grief cycle. If the grief cycle is that of people moving forward in life and you being stuck in this moment that you can't seem to move past. No matter how good someone is to you, the way Kari and her family were, or even my own family, you end up spending a lot of time alone, because everyone is living, you my friend are just existing. Barely getting through the day.

You are in a strange place of survival. It is like getting thrown in the deep end of the water, not knowing how to swim, with no life preservers around to grasp. So, you paddle like crazy trying to get to something solid to hold onto, all the while going under the water, gulping water, bobbing up, gasping for air. You try to find anything just not to drown in the body of pain that has consumed you and everything around you.

I've heard the cliché that drowning is one of the most peaceful ways to die, but there was nothing peaceful about the drowning I was doing emotionally. Words elude me here.

You don't get it until you go through it. Most people who have not experienced this kind of pain think they know how you should feel. They have empathy to a degree, but they don't really know how you feel, even if they think they do. Sometimes they will tell you what they think you should be feeling or when you should be feeling it or not be feeling it anymore. They stand in judgment even without meaning to do so. The timeline that is in many people's minds isn't something you can adhere to. Sometimes I would be triggered in some way, and end up right back at the beginning, with the same old feelings of shame, guilt, embarrassment, anger, and heartache.

I remember about six months after sentencing, I had to go to the police station to pick up Christopher's and Drake's personal belongings. I went in to get the boxes and the female officer asked me, "What's your son's deal?"

I replied with, "What do you mean?"

She then said, "Well, acting how he did, to place himself in prison. What's his issue?"

I said, "Well, I don't know how he acted being that I don't have the police report, so I don't know if he acted in self defence, if it was five guys against the two of them, like I heard."

Then I added, "I do not know, that if my son didn't have a knife to protect himself, if he would be alive. I don't know if that is the only reason he is, being that you seem to have all the information why you don't tell me. I do know that if he was beaten badly or to death that we wouldn't be having this conversation, so unless you have information for me that you can share to enlighten me on what you think my son's deal or issue is, I have nothing really to say, except for can I please have the boys' belongings that I came in for."

This incident might sound insignificant; however, I was furious. I remember walking out, getting to the car, looking at my husband, and starting to cry while telling him what happened. Then I let the tears fall, allowing myself to break down in the car. I wasn't really furious, I was hurt, and I was sad, it was just easier to be angry when self-preserving. Through the sobs I asked my husband, "Why did she feel she had a right to talk to me in that condescending way? Why did she think it would be okay to talk down about my son to me? Or was it because my son had left a distaste in her mouth, that she felt that it was ok for her to spread her disdain onto me? Did she feel she could paint us with the same brush?"

You would hope in her professional career choice that she would be better. Maybe she was bullied as a child and this was her way of getting back some power and control. Maybe she picked this job because it allowed her to feel superior over others. Maybe she was and still is a bully. Possibly she thought it ok to belittle someone who she viewed as weak or less than to make herself feel better. Or did she feel because I was his mom that I was part of what happened, like so many people I overheard talking about the situation? Did she feel I was responsible for what he did, and I should be punished for his actions?

As parents, we tend to feel responsible for our kids and their actions. We do it when we are proud of them with smiles; it's not the same when it is attached to a less desirable behaviour. I have seen this firsthand and lived it myself.

How did she feel that it was ok to talk to me that way, to put my family down to make me feel small, to purposely shame me?

The long and short of it all is that I don't know what HER DEAL is. However, I hope she gets help for it and can learn to be a better human. Understand that to serve and protect is a pretty broad spectrum and in no way did she serve me or protect me. In fact she is one that inflicted unnecessary pain and did a disservice because I have no respect for her as an RCMP. It left a pretty awful taste in my mouth and though I work at letting it go, it still seems to be a bit of an issue for me. I don't know if it has to do with her self-righteous behaviour or possibly because I had a higher expectation because she was part of the police force, or maybe because I was already so broken and her behaviour was just too much for me, so I filed it away for a time that I could deal with it better and that time just has not come yet.

The shame that comes along with one of these interactions puts you farther down the rabbit hole of darkness than you already are. You tend to go more within, spend more time at home, more time alone. I do not know if she was aware of the damage she placed upon my broken heart, aware or not, the damage was done.

This is just one example of the kinds of things that I encountered each and every day. The perception people have of you, the things they say can really affect you when you are already vulnerable and broken. They may not be aware but that does not stop the extra damage they add to your heart and mind.

You will come across some people that will tell you that maybe this is a good thing and maybe he will learn. I am not sure if they mean for his mistakes or his punishment, it makes no difference, hearing someone say it still sends me over the top. What was he to learn? What exactly did they think he was going to get educated in from being in prison? Did they think his life skills would be enhanced? Was he going to learn better math, English? Was he going to learn how to be kind, to be a gentleman? What...what did they think he would learn...it is still a question that I ponder every so often, wondering if they think he has learned whatever it was that they thought he was supposed to learn. Whatever they expected or had in their minds for him to learn while incarcerated, he did not.

He learned things, for sure: how to comply, how to adapt to small living quarters, how to manipulate better; the point being people say shitty things, and in the statement of maybe he will learn, they think that the system will make him make better choices, that imprisonment will teach him and my point is it does not. Most criminals will go back to prison because life is hard and once you have spent time in prison with structure and condition that you can comply with, it is easier than life itself. They don't learn skills to be better people, how to cope and deal with life so they do not learn what people are implying.

If they thought he learned not to behave in the same way that got him arrested, the answer would be no. Everyone learns that at the moment they screw up. It is no different than when you're speeding; you know you're speeding, but you do it, until you get caught and you have to pay the fine or your car gets towed. You know…you know right then and there you're in the wrong. Like doing your taxes and finding loops or better deals, you don't care until you get audited. Or running a red light, until you hit another car. We all know the moment we screw up, especially when we get caught or hurt another.

The other comment that was my "favourite" was, "Maybe prison is the best place for him."WTF, a.k.a., what the fuck!!! Yep, every single time that would go through my mind. Every time someone said it, every time to this day I still think that. What in people's minds, much like the police officer, made them think that this was an okay statement to say to me, his mother. How do they justify talking to me and saying such a thing? So, for those of you that are still thinking that maybe it's the best place and what am I so cranky about. I will break it down for you.

I am his mom…I birthed him…I raised him…I love him…I want nothing but the best for him. I want him to live a full good life...I want for him to be the best human he can be. Do you think for one minute that I believe that best place for my child is prison?

It's no different than telling someone who has lost their child to death that their child is in a better place. No parent believes that their child is in a better place if they are no longer living. Believing in God or not, everyone wants their child to be living with them, not finding peace and harmony in Heaven. And no parent ever believes that the best place for their child is in prison, EVER!

I am not saying that Drake or Christopher didn't have to deal with the consequences of their choices. They did absolutely. I'm not say that being imprisoned wasn't the deserved punishment; but what I am saying is that it's certainly not the best place for them to learn to be healthy members of society.

It became harder and harder to socialize for many reasons. One was comments like these, which caused the emotions to wash over me, both sadness and anger. And you run into the people who want to educate you on how you *ought* to be feeling, how you should be doing so much better than you are. They tell you that it's not you in prison, so why don't you just let it go? Or get over it.

With each statement or comment, you find yourself closing up, and with that self-protective closing-up there comes a change on how you deal with people. I didn't even realize how dark I was becoming, or how isolated. But you start questioning if you have the ability to deal with people at all.

It was such a strange place to be in all aspects of my life. Even if something good happened, it wasn't significant enough to make a real impact. It seemed like people around me were moving forward, their day-to-day lives were changing and evolving and I was stuck in some sort of time warp. Like the movie *Groundhog Day*, I was unable to move beyond a certain point of Drake and Christopher being arrested. Well, they all had new developments in the day, mine consisted of the same; nothing changed, nothing moved, nothing shifted. It was like I was crippled by carrying this burden and loss with me daily. The weight of it so heavy that it left me feeling depleted and exhausted. There was no energy left to try to explain how I felt and there wasn't much else for me to talk about. Nothing for me to bring to the table for normal conversation, which led to me spending more and more time alone.

The boys going to prison altered my life. I wanted someone to care about me, my feelings, my emotions, my heartache; I wanted to know that I really mattered. I realize that people are unable to show up while you are in a deep state of grief. Partially because they do not understand and do not know how to show up, and partially because the loneliest walk you will ever take is the one down the road of grief.

There were some positive things that came from this time: learning to paint, plant, write, go for counselling, learning about myself and my emotions. I also gained insight into my thoughts about parenting, friendships, and family. I learned that while you are dealing with a broken heart you go through a swing of emotions; your tolerance for things is minimal. You don't really deal with things internally; you look for validation from others. Because you can't deal with your emotions, you want someone else to tell you that you're okay. At the end of the day, happiness is still an inside job.

It was easier to be angry than was to explain my sadness. There is a cycle of grief, and I was caught in it. I could not move past a certain part of it, no matter how hard I tried. I think this happens to everyone, though I only have my situations to go with. Moving through the grief of my best friend's death was different than moving through the grief of not having my children in my life daily for a couple years. I counselled like crazy, but it still did not move me through the cycle or create the difference I had hoped. Logically I under-stood counselling was great for that; emotionally I was stuck.

I was the only outside voice and advocate for the boys. I was always on the defence and maybe that is why I got a bit stuck. Maybe because you're unable to process any farther. May-be because you can't imagine going through a day without them, so you just stop because it is far too much for you to emotionally handle. I do not honestly know. I do know that some days were worse and some days slightly better, but I was still stuck.

It's like a constant nagging that something is wrong. You never forget that you can't just pick up the phone to call your sons or stop by to tell them about something that happened in your day. They never leave your thoughts. You could be doing something so random and it's like your heart just can't handle another reminder of the absence. Driving by the school they attended, seeing one of their friends, sitting at the beach, watching a sunset, the snow falling, getting dressed, or brushing your teeth. When energy was hard to find to make it out of bed, to walk to the bathroom to brush your teeth. You end up looking in the mirror and as soon as you make eye contact with that person getting ready to brush their teeth, you break down in uncontrollable sobs and you slide to the ground and stay there sobbing until you can find the energy to climb back into bed. Screw it to washing your face, brushing your teeth and hair; find the salvation of the bed. Let the sorrow of the woman you made eye contact with in the mirror, the one that you recognize but feel so separated from, the one that you will allow to sob because you just saw the deep, deep sorrow of pain in her eyes and because you recognized her sorrow; you allowed no judgment or justification, you saw the unbearable pain, that is why you looked away so quickly in hopes that it wouldn't break you, but it did and you hope that she weeps so much that she passes out from exhaustion and pray to God that she will find a little tiny bit of peace in sleep, because that is the only peace you will get for a very long time. Some associations are easy to understand, others are not.

Everything that you have to do just takes a bit more from you. Getting out of bed, getting dressed, enlisting the energy to try to convince yourself that you need to do these things, that's exhausting. The amount of time it takes for you to talk yourself into going to your appointment, following through with connecting with your friend, the energy and time it takes you to mentally prepare yourself to go out into the world and pretend that you are okay—all of this is completely fucking exhausting.

It wasn't until the night before Drake was to be released that I realized just how dark and narrow my world had become. I had been so caught up in the heartache, the anger, that it was all consuming. Feeling misunderstood, people unable to relate to my emotional pain, and feeling so powerless and lost I ended up not wanting to do much of anything. Lie in bed, not talk, not socialize, not feel; my world had become cold and lonely. The ugly truth of it all is you are so traumatized by your emotional pain that you cannot see any light. But the night before your light is to be released you realize how heavy the burden has actually been.

EPILOGUE

As I write this, I try to think back on some things that were positive that happened while Drake was in prison, and my initial reaction is nothing. However, reflecting back I learned that you will not die from a broken heart alone, though I do understand how people can get consumed by this kind of grief and pain.

I learned that things change, although you may not see the change right away. You change with it, unknowing or knowing. I learned that I have no control over anyone else's life and at times not even my own, the only thing that I have control of is how I choose to react to it all.

I also learned that there is not a lot of help for young boys or men who need it. I learned that there is not a lot of support for certain types of situations in life, so sometimes you must be the change you want to see. And I learned that a lot of people are walking around wounded and feeling helpless.

I found out that I have a voice with a lot to say and that come hell or high water I was going to speak about my boys, because this situation was not going to define us for the rest of our lives.

Drake and Christopher both used to tell me that they thought their imprisonment and life choices were harder on me than on them, and they may very well be right. We have images in our minds about who and what our children are; we project our beliefs and ideals onto them. We have dreams and goals for ourselves, as well as for them.

So, in the end, I can say I have gained from this heartbreak, I have more empathy and care, that I have gained knowledge and understanding. Along with belief in myself and my own strength. Have I fully recovered? No, and I am not sure I ever will. I will never be the same person I was before the boys went to prison, though I do want to say, as hard as it has been, I am grateful to be the person I am today. I will always worry about Drake and Christopher, as I do all the children I helped raise and I call mine, as well as my grandchildren.

I want the best for them; I want them to be the best versions of themselves. It has been one of the most challenging yet satisfying things to love them and I can honestly say that I love them unconditionally. I know maybe people say they love unconditionally, and I believe they think they do. I know I did, however one never really knows until they are challenged to prove it.

Is it easier when life is going according to our idea of what we think it ought to look like? Sure.

When what you believe or imagined to be true gets shattered along with your heart in a blink of an eye, and you still love the person who broke it, you still want the best for that person, despite the heartache created.

You love your children despite the heartache, the challenges. You love them for who and what they are today, right now. You have to let go of what you believed would happen or what you wanted them to be. You accept that this is who and what they are, and you love them anyway.

I do not hang my head in shame or embarrassment for anything that happened or happens now. And I do not avoid talking about any of our current situations in life. I no longer keep my emotions or struggles over the last seven years to myself, fearful of what people will think or how they will judge me. Instead, I speak freely about my pain and that I am still healing bits and pieces of me. As heartbreaking as this all was, I think I became a better person because of it. I know what it means to love and let go.

That said, even today I can get caught up in the judgment of others when I talk about the journey of the boys going to prison, about Christopher being on the streets today, and all the struggles I've been through with them due to mental health and addiction. I am sad about the constraints of fear that have restricted the hearts of others. Everyone is on their own journey. I know what it means to hold space for someone, even if that person is not following the path we'd hoped. Chris, Drake, and I are each on our own paths, entirely separate, yet together with love in my heart, a heart that is no longer behind bars.

ACKNOWLEDGMENTS

To Book Launchers for helping me and guiding me in creating my first book, for helping me through the long, long process, and for giving me feedback and tools to allow this project to come to fruition. Thank you. Thank you. Thank you.

To my family and friends who loved me through it at various stages and those who were lovingly consistent. I would like to mention all of you; however, I have a limited amount of space, so please, if you're not mentioned, I am terribly sorry. I hope that I let you know I am grateful for you often and you understand the whys.

Kair Jonker—without her I would have been so extremely

lost in the beginning of this journey. She gave and shared gifts, such as knowledge of pain and grieving, acceptance and understanding, and the expression of art through paint. Her kind heart and loving family helped me in so many ways.

Cheri Brown, for letting me be, letting me cry, letting me be crazy, letting me be out of control and still accepting me. I know it was challenging at times. ☺

Kara Phillips, Christa Smith, and Victoria Bohati for listening to me over and over and over again.

Cathy Platz and the ferry clan, Tanya, Kristina, Carisa, Patrice, Caron, Juanita, and Claude. Different stages and different times for some of you. And for you, Cath, you just never gave up on me since Grade 7–8, something like that. I'm grateful. You couldn't fully understand the pain; however, you tried to stop me from drowning in sorrow.

MG, for showing up and supporting not only myself but Kaylee as well, for venturing to visitations even though it created a bit of turbulence, and for loving us, all of us, the boys as well. We are blessed to have you in our world.

Sean, for reading and re-reading and reading some more.

IM (Maverick) for helping me choose photos, layout, and so much more.

Jenna LeFebvre thank you for the amazing photography section and letting me show my best self to the world.

Dad, for encouraging me to stay strong and speak my piece even when you didn't agree with what I had to say. Mom, for allowing me to be angry and understanding the rage. Supporting me in the crazy that was my life. My siblings, my aunts and uncles, my cousins, their spouses, and their children for showing up when I needed support. Mark Britt, Dianne, and JC, for loving me, not always liking my behavior, however, loving me none the less.

Auntie Sue, Uncle Bill, Deb and Mike Roberts, Greg Freethy, and Corrine Freethy, thanks for letting me crash the Sunday funday dinner. You guys were my first support of a broken heart. You left an everlasting positive impact. I cannot graciously thank you enough.

Adam and Michelle Day, for being great godparents and loving us through all the tough times. Thanks for joining the tribe Michelle, it wouldn't be the same without you. XO

Jason Mester, for picking me up off the ground. Although we had our struggles, you showed up to support me when I needed it.

Kaylee Britt, my pook. What else can I say. Love you infinity.

Drake Britt, for the photo. While incarcerated he paid a guard to take a photo of him sending me some love. That is what we used for the cover. Also with him and Christopher in prison, it inspired the painting that is in between the chapters.

To all my children and add ons, Christopher, Josh (Detroit), Pascal, girl Alex, boy Alex, Tater tots (Tait), Dakota, Stacy baby, Payton, it was a trying time, and I do not think I completely lost my mind—but it was close. ☺

To each and every one of you who have come and gone out of our family home, those of you who still refer to me as Mama B, thank you for giving me the gift of loving you, evolving, developing, and helping me grow into the parent I am today. Thank you for allowing me to lecture you and love you unconditionally. I am truly blessed to have you all. XO